detox dieting

detox
dieting

Over 50 healthy
and delicious recipes
to cleanse your system

Consultant Editor:
Nicola Graimes

LORENZ BOOKS

First published in 2002 by Lorenz Books

© Anness Publishing Limited 2000, 2001

Lorenz Books is an imprint of
Anness Publishing Limited
Hermes House
88–89 Blackfriars Road
London SE1 8HA

www.lorenzbooks.com

This edition distributed in Canada by Raincoast Books
9050 Shaughnessy Street, Vancouver BC, V6P 6E5

A CIP catalogue record is available from the British Library

Publisher: Joanna Lorenz
Executive Editor: Linda Fraser
Project Editor: Susannah Blake
Editorial Reader: Hayley Kerr
Production Controller: Don Campaniello
Introduction: Nicola Graimes
Recipes: Catherine Atkinson, Angela Boggiano, Carla Capalbo, Trish Davies,
Patrizia Diemling, Joanna Farrow, Nicola Graimes, Deh-Ta Hsiung,
Christine Ingram, Lesley Mackey, Kathy Man, Sally Mansfield,
Maggie Mayhew, Steven Wheeler, Kate Whiteman and Jeni Wright
Photography: Janine Hosegood, with additional pictures by Nicky Dowey,
James Duncan, Ian Garlick, Michelle Garrett, Amanda Heywood,
Dave Jordan, Dave King, William Lingwood, Thomas Odulate and Sam Stowell;
Image Bank (p7t); Tony Stone Images (pp6, 7b and 8); and Superstock (p9)
Designer: Ian Sandom
Nutritional Analysis: Clare Brain
Indexer: Hilary Bird

Also published as *Healthy Eating Library The Detox Diet Cookbook*.

Printed and bound in China

1 3 5 7 9 10 8 6 4 2

The diets and information in this book are not intended to replace advice from a qualified
practitioner, doctor or dietician. Always consult your health practitioner before adopting
any of the suggestions in this book.

NOTES
For all recipes, quantities are given in both metric and imperial measures
and, where appropriate, measures are also given in standard cups and spoons.
Follow one set, but not a mixture, because they are not interchangeable.

Standard spoon and cup measures are level.
1 tsp = 5ml, 1 tbsp = 15ml, 1 cup = 250ml/8fl oz

Australian standard tablespoons are 20ml. Australian readers should
use 3 tsp in place of 1 tbsp for measuring small quantities

CONTENTS

INTRODUCTION

If you constantly feel tired, find it difficult to get to sleep and equally difficult to get up in the morning, regularly suffer from headaches or indigestion, and generally feel below par, you could be suffering from toxic overload and may benefit from a detox. We all want optimum health and mental clarity, and a detox can help you on your way by giving your body a spring clean, boosting energy levels and filling you with a zest for life. Even the healthiest among us may benefit from an occasional detox and enjoy the extra boost of energy and vitality that it can provide.

WHAT ARE TOXINS?

Toxins come in various different guises and there is nothing new about them. What is new is the quantity and nature of the toxins we face today. Toxins are harmful substances that pollute and irritate our bodies, putting a strain on the efficiency of our vital organs. The body is a finely tuned machine that is designed to do battle with these unwanted substances, but its efficiency is dependent on age and health, with the young and healthy being in the best position to fight toxins. When the system becomes overburdened and unable to cope, toxins can build up in the body. This build-up is likely to have a negative impact on your health and general well-being, affecting the body's key functions, such as digestion and circulation. It has even been suggested that toxin overload is linked with some of the most serious diseases, including cancer and heart disease.

WHERE DO TOXINS COME FROM?

Toxins bombard us from all sides – externally, from the environment, and internally, produced in the body itself. Unless you decide to live in a sterile bubble, it is virtually impossible to avoid harmful toxins. Everyday activities that we usually think of as being healthy, such as a walk in the park or eating a piece of fruit, are often actually subjecting us to toxins. It has been estimated that, on average, we eat or drink about 3.75 litres/1 gallon of pesticides (found on fresh foods), take in 5kg/11¼lb of chemical food additives, and breathe in 2g of solid pollution every year.

Above: We are constantly faced with toxins from the air we breathe and the food that we eat. A detox can help to improve your energy levels and lift your mood.

WHAT IS A DETOX?

The principle of a detox is simply to heal the body through cleansing. The body has its own set of natural detoxification processes, which work to eliminate the toxins that are ingested everyday. A detox aims to aid and enhance these natural processes. By reducing the amount of food normally eaten and choosing foods that can cleanse the body, a detox diet will provide your digestive system with a well-earned rest, allowing it to concentrate on healing itself and eliminating toxins. The different approaches to detoxing vary greatly in terms of what you have to do and how rigidly you need to stick to a given programme's guidelines.

The most stringent form of detox is a fast. This method encourages the body's natural detoxifying processes by replacing food with water, herbal teas and fresh juices. Fasts are usually only recommended for a short length of time, although they can be undertaken for longer during an extreme fast. Claims have been made that long fasts can be used to cure some major illnesses, such as cancer, but it is very important not to follow such a radical diet without seeking the advice of a qualified practitioner or doctor.

Slightly less severe than a fast is a mild detox. A mild detox can range from just drinking water, herbal teas and juices to a diet that also includes raw foods and salads, brown rice and lightly cooked vegetables and soups.

By far the gentlest method of detoxing, which is much less radical than either fasting or a mild detox, is a cleansing diet. A cleansing diet includes a wider range of foods, as well as juices and herbal teas, and can be used as a long-term detox. Important healing foods, such as grains, beans, nuts, seeds and a range of sea vegetables, play a vital role in cleansing diets.

BENEFITS OF A DETOX

A detox is thought to cleanse and rejuvenate the body, improve the circulation and metabolism, and strengthen the immune system. It can also improve the condition of your skin, hair and nails, and slow down the aging process. As well as the physical benefits, a detox can improve your ability to cope with stress, declutter your mind and lift your mood, leaving you feeling relaxed and energized.

THE EFFECTS OF THE ENVIRONMENT

With every breath, you inhale pollutants that are in the air: traffic fumes, cigarette smoke, and fumes from office ventilation systems and industrial pollution. However, your home and place of work can be equally detrimental to your health. Indoor air pollutants range from those that come from computers and air conditioning to those from dust, cleaning fluids, dyes, glues, paint, detergents, insulation and soft furnishings. Pollutants come from the most surprising sources: deodorants contain aluminium, and toothpaste can include ammonia, ethanol and mineral oil.

The number of people suffering from asthma has risen by staggering proportions over the last ten years. Many attribute this increase to a rise in airborne pollution. Other symptoms that have been blamed on poor air quality include a weakened immune system, lung disease, allergies, respiratory problems and even cancer.

How to reduce exposure to toxins

• Avoid walking in highly polluted parts of town.
• If you live in a city, try to escape occasionally to the countryside or coast.

Above: The average person consumes about a gallon of pesticides every year.

• Always wear a mask if you cycle in the city.
• Buy eco-friendly cleaners, washing powder and washing-up liquid.
• Recycle and buy recycled products.
• Don't be one of the estimated 7 million people who turn off their television using a remote control. This lazy habit helps to generate an additional 200,000 tons of carbon dioxide each year.

THE EFFECTS OF FOOD

In a recent study, 46 per cent of fruit and vegetables in the UK contained pesticide residues. A group of pesticides with the general name organophosphates were found in dangerously high quantities in carrots and celery, while chemical residues found in grapes were equally worrying. There has been increasing concern about genetically modified food and irradiation, and tap water can contain heavy metals, DDT, asbestos, arsenic, and nitrates and nitrites from fertilizers.

Food allergies and intolerances have reached epidemic proportions. Skin and respiratory problems, headaches, hyperactivity, antisocial behaviour and anxiety attacks, as well as life-threatening diseases such as cancer, have all been linked to dietary pollution.

How to reduce consumption of toxins

• Buy organic foods whenever possible.
• Avoid drinking tap water – opt for filtered or mineral water.
• Reduce your intake of processed and packaged foods.
• Cut back on the amount of sweet, fatty and salty foods you eat.
• Always wash and peel non-organic fruit and vegetables.
• Avoid eating dairy products and meat too often.
• Keep your intake of tea, coffee and fizzy drinks to a minimum.
• Read labels carefully to avoid artificial additives and genetically modified ingredients.

ARE YOU SUFFERING FROM TOXIC OVERLOAD?

Check how toxic you are by answering the questions below. The more questions that you answer "yes" to, the more toxic you are likely to be and the more likely you are to benefit from a detox.

❏ Are you constantly tired?
❏ Is your skin spotty or dull?
❏ Are you constipated?
❏ Do you have dark circles under your eyes?
❏ Are your eyes and hair dull?
❏ Do you suffer from headaches?
❏ Do you have aches and pains in your joints?
❏ Do you suffer from high levels of catarrh and sinus problems?
❏ Do you suffer from night sweats?
❏ Do you suffer from flatulence?
❏ Do you suffer from bloating and water retention?
❏ Do you have cellulite?
❏ Do you have problems sleeping?
❏ Do you have problems maintaining concentration?
❏ Do you suffer from frequent mood changes, including depression, anxiety or an inability to concentrate?
❏ Do your muscles ache for no reason?
❏ Do you suffer from skin rashes or eczema?
❏ Do you suffer from stress?
❏ Do you suffer from irritable bowel syndrome?

How the Body Fights Toxins

The body is a remarkable piece of organic engineering, working to eliminate undesirable substances via the skin, lungs, kidneys, liver, digestive system and lymphatic system. When the body is not firing on all cylinders, it tends to store toxins instead of eliminating them.

The Liver

This is our most complex organ and handles almost everything that enters the body. It has thousands of functions, including the removal of toxins from the bloodstream. Harmful substances are neutralized and passed from the liver to the intestines in bile. The liver also produces a supply of long-term energy for the body, by converting the energy from food into the metabolic nutrients that are needed for cells to function efficiently.

Optimum health depends on the efficient functioning of the liver. If the liver becomes overloaded with toxins, they are stored there and in fat cells throughout the body. Signs that may indicate an unhappy liver range from headaches, cellulite, irritable bowel syndrome, poor digestion, bloating, depression and mood changes to the more serious problems of diabetes, hepatitis and cirrhosis.

The Kidneys

The main role of the kidneys is to filter toxins in the blood and eliminate them in urine. They also play a key role in processing the by-products of eating and are responsible for regulating the amount of fluid in the body and recycling nutrients for further use.

The Lymphatic System

This system carries toxins, unwanted waste, dead cells and excess fluid to the lymph nodes, where the waste is filtered before being passed into the bloodstream. Cellulite, poor circulation and a weakened immune system are all signs that the lymphatic system is not functioning properly. High levels of toxins are believed to slow down your lymphatic system.

Above: A walk in the fresh air revitalizes the whole body.

The Lungs

When we breathe, the lungs deal with airborne pollutants, such as carbon monoxide. They allow oxygen to enter the bloodstream and waste products to be removed as carbon dioxide.

Correct breathing is essential if the body's metabolism and organs are to work properly. However, many of us do not inhale enough oxygen and so do not expel all the unwanted waste gases. Catarrh, blocked sinuses and a constant runny nose are signs of a poorly functioning respiratory system.

The Digestive System

Your health is often governed by your digestive system. Everything you eat travels from the stomach to the intestines, where nutrients are absorbed and waste is eliminated via the bowels. Food is broken down by digestive enzymes and "friendly" bacteria in the gut. If these are out of sync due to poor diet, stress, overuse of antibiotics, food intolerances or toxin overload, food remains semi-digested, and problems, such as constipation, leaky gut, irritable bowel syndrome, nausea, and bloating, arise. Food itself can also become toxic if not digested properly.

THE SKIN
This is the body's largest organ. Every pore eliminates waste, and sweat and the sebaceous glands help to remove toxins. The skin reflects what is happening inside our bodies. If we are stressed, run down or have over-indulged, this can show up in a dull, lifeless complexion, or as rashes, spots, blotches and blemishes.

HOW TO BOOST YOUR VITAL ORGANS
Like a car, the body benefits from a regular service to ensure it runs efficiently and has sufficient energy to fight toxins. There are a number of simple, common-sense steps that can help to improve the overall functioning of your vital organs.

THE LIVER
• Drink plenty of water – at least eight glasses a day.
• Eat plenty of fresh fruit and veg-etables, in particular apples, garlic, beetroot, carrots, broccoli, cabbage, artichokes, asparagus, ginger, green leafy vegetables, alfalfa and bitter leaves, such as dandelion, as well as wholegrains, nuts, seeds and beans.
• Avoid processed, fried, salty and sugary foods, as well as foods to which you may be allergic.
• Try to eat mainly organic foods.
• Cut down on alcohol and caffeine.

Above: Regular exercise aids the effective functioning of your internal organs.

• Exercise regularly.
• Liver-boosting supplements can help to neutralize free radicals that damage cells. Try an antioxidant supplement containing betacarotene, vitamins C and E and selenium.

THE KIDNEYS
• Drink plenty of water – at least eight glasses a day.
• Reduce your intake of animal pro-tein foods, such as meat and dairy products, as these put a strain on the workings of the kidneys.
• Cut down on alcohol.

THE LYMPHATIC SYSTEM
• Exercise regularly.
• Stimulate the lymphatic system by exfoliating and skin-brushing.
• Have a massage to encourage the efficiency of the lymphatic system.

THE LUNGS
Use this exercise to check that you are breathing correctly.
1 Lie with your back on the floor, bending your knees and placing your feet on the floor a comfortable distance from your buttocks. Rest your hands flat on your stomach, just below your ribs.
2 Breathe in slowly through your nose, filling your lungs – feel your stomach expand. The lower part of your stomach should rise first and you should feel the breath slowly moving up your body. If your chest moves first, you are breathing incorrectly and are not using your diaphragm – this is known as "shallow breathing".
3 Exhale slowly through your nostrils, emptying your lungs – notice your abdomen flattening.

Above: Water is the key to the effective functioning of every organ.

THE DIGESTIVE SYSTEM
• Only eat when you are hungry and try not to overeat.
• Take time over meals, chewing each mouthful properly and slowly.
• Do not drink too much with meals as this can dilute the digestive juices.
• Start the day with fruit juices or fruit to boost your digestive system.
• Herbal teas, such as camomile or peppermint, can be soothing.
• Improve the condition of the gut by eating natural live yogurt.

SKIN
• Drink plenty of water – at least eight glasses a day.
• Eat plenty of fresh vegetables and fruit, preferably raw or juiced.
• Eat foods rich in betacarotene, vitamins C and E, B vitamins, calcium, iron and essential fatty acids.
• Boost your circulation by exercising and skin-brushing.
• Get plenty of sleep and fresh air.

FOODS TO AVOID

Diet is the key to a healthy body and lively mind. Eating a wide range of fresh and nutritious wholefoods will result in a positive response from your body. However, certain foods are thought to hinder your body's ability to cleanse itself. These foods should be excluded from your diet during a detox and, ideally, should be kept to a minimum after a detox. Although a poor diet suppresses the efficient workings of the body, the body has an amazing ability to heal itself. By paying more attention to what you eat, you can often counteract imbalances surprisingly quickly.

PROCESSED AND REFINED FOODS

Modern methods of food production are guilty of overprocessing many of our foods, which means that many of the natural nutrients are destroyed. Valuable fibre, vitamins and minerals are stripped away, leaving food that, in nutritional terms, is a poor substitute for the original. Some manufacturers replace these lost nutrients with supplements, but it is debatable as to whether or not these are in a form that the body can assimilate.

Large-scale farming and food production has also seen widespread use of chemicals, preservatives and irradiation, as well as the introduction of genetically modified crops.

Although it is difficult to completely avoid processed and packaged foods, try to opt for organic wholefoods whenever possible.

Above: Consuming excessive amounts of alcohol can inhibit the absorption of essential vitamins and minerals and places unnecessary strain on the liver.

ALCOHOL

The occasional glass of wine does little harm, and is even reputed to help in the fight against coronary heart disease. However, alcohol is virtually worthless in terms of nutritional value and, if drunk in excess, is positively harmful.

Heavy drinking harms the liver and places unnecessary strain on its normal day-to-day functioning. It also depletes nutrients, such as vitamins A and C, the B vitamins, magnesium, zinc and the essential fatty acids, and leads to severe dehydration.

Modern methods of producing alcoholic drinks often mean that your average glass of wine, beer or spirit will contain chemical pesticides, colourants and other harmful additives, which will put further strain on the liver.

CAFFEINE

This powerful stimulant works on the nervous system and is highly addictive. It is most commonly found in coffee, tea, chocolate, colas and some fizzy soft drinks.

Coffee contains the most caffeine, at around 65mg for an average cup of instant, while tea averages 40mg per cup. Chocolate, colas and fizzy drinks tend to contain slightly less.

Consuming an excessive amount of caffeine (for example, drinking over six cups of coffee a day) can result in irritability, insomnia, headaches, migraine and high blood pressure. It can also reduce the body's ability to absorb vitamins and minerals.

Before embarking on a detox programme, big coffee and tea drinkers should try to reduce their intake gradually. Sudden withdrawal can cause the same symptoms as

Above: Processed and packaged foods are best avoided in favour of organic foods.

Above: Try to drink less coffee, or switch to coffee substitutes or herbal teas.

drinking too much. Swapping to decaffeinated tea or coffee may help in the short-term; try to find brands that remove caffeine using the water filtration method, rather than chemical solvents. Better still, try using coffee substitutes, which may be flavoured with dandelion or roasted grains, or swap to green tea or herbal infusions.

DAIRY PRODUCTS

These foods, which include butter, cheese and milk, are high in saturated fats and are best avoided when detoxing. Saturated fats slow down the lymphatic system, which is responsible for removing toxins from the body.

Margerines should also be avoided as they can contain hydrogenated or trans fats, which are produced during processing. In the long-term, unsalted, organic butter or non-hydrogenated margarines are preferable.

Cow's milk can contain growth promoters, hormones and antibiotics, which put a strain on the whole body.

The only exception is natural live yogurt, which has a soothing, nurturing effect on the digestive system. It can also help to keep up levels of healthy bacteria in the gut.

Above: Saturated fats found in red meat and dairy products slow down the lymphatic system and its ability to get rid of toxins.

Above: Meat and fish should be avoided during a detox programme.

MEAT AND FISH

Even for non-vegetarians, meat should only make up a small part of the diet and should be excluded altogether during a detox. Most people will usually benefit from cutting down on their meat intake. It is notoriously difficult to digest and, unless organic, may include traces of growth promoters, hormones and preservatives that are used in meat production. It is also a major source of saturated fat.

Fish is much easier to digest and is lower in saturated fat than meat but unless, like tuna, it is from the deep oceans, it can harbour unwanted pollutants. Farmed fish should also be avoided, as they are routinely fed antibiotics and other additives.

WHEAT

Foods based on wheat, such as bread and pasta, are best avoided when embarking on a detox programme. Wheat is a common allergen. Many people also suffer from coeliac disease, which is an intolerance to the gluten found in wheat. Wheat bran can inhibit the absorption of some of our most important nutrients and can irritate the lining of the intestines.

SALT AND SUGAR

Most people eat too much salt. This is largely due to food manufacturing and processing, which adds large amounts of salt to the foods that we regard as everyday staples, such as bread, cereals and canned goods.

Excess salt overloads the kidneys and leads to water retention, as well as increasing blood pressure. Fresh or dried herbs, spices and fresh lemon juice are excellent alternatives to salt, adding plenty of flavour without any of the detrimental effects of salt.

If you are in the habit of sprinkling salt liberally over everything you eat, the only real alternative is to re-educate your palate. You will soon find that salt starts to become increasingly unpalatable and that foods can taste better without.

Sweet foods such as biscuits and cakes that contain large amounts of refined sugar can upset the balance of blood sugars in the body. They supply little in the way of nourishment and can suppress the appetite. Natural sugars, which are found in fresh and dried fruit, are much kinder on the system and provide the body with vital nutrients and fibre.

Above: Cakes and biscuits contain large amounts of fat and refined sugar, which can upset blood sugar levels.

THE DETOX SUPERFOODS

There are many foods that can help to cleanse your body and encourage the elimination of toxins, thereby improving your general health and vitality. The following foods supply valuable nutrients and fibre, as well as offering healing and curative properties. They are essential when detoxing and should be at the heart of every long-term healthy, cleansing diet.

Left: Fresh fruit is the ultimate detox food, providing a powerhouse of vital nutrients.

Apples
These common fruits contain malic and tartaric acid, which boost digestion and remove impurities from the liver. Their cleansing properties are further enhanced by their high fibre and pectin content, which help to remove toxins and purify the system. Apples are also an excellent source of betacarotene and vitamin C and contain fructose, which provides a steady stream of energy.

Pears
Eaten regularly, pears are said to ensure a clear complexion and glossy hair. Their high water content means that pears are an effective diuretic and laxative. They also contain vitamin C, potassium, fibre and pectin.

Grapes
These are one of the most effective detoxifiers and are often chosen for a one-day mono-diet. They are said to relieve constipation and treat kidney, liver, digestive and skin disorders, and are good for the blood. Black grapes

FRUIT
Packed with vitamins, minerals, fibre, amino acids and enzymes, fruit, particularly raw fruit, should feature as a major staple in any detox.

The rich fibre and water content of fruit means that it is a perfect internal cleanser. The fibre binds with toxins and the water helps to flush them out. Fruit pectin has been shown to bind with heavy metals, such as lead, helping to carry them from the body.

Lemons
As well as providing vitamin C, lemon juice is a powerful cleanser, astringent and antiseptic, stimulating the liver and gallbladder. A glass of hot water with freshly squeezed lemon juice is the ideal start to a detox day.

Oranges
Freshly juiced oranges stimulate the digestion and tone the system. Oranges contain high levels of vitamin C, a powerful antioxidant. These help to protect the body against harmful free radicals, inhibiting those that lead to premature aging and reducing the risk of cancer and heart disease. Vitamin C can also increase iron absorption.

Grapefruits
These fruits stimulate the digestive system, making them perfect for breakfast or at the start of a meal. They are rich in vitamin C and are a good source of betacarotene, calcium, phosphorus and potassium. Vitamin C and pectin have been found to help control cholesterol levels.

Above: Lemons are a rich source of cleansing vitamin C.

Above: Cherries are reputed to relieve arthritis and constipation.

are the most potent. However, grapes are often sprayed with a heavy dose of pesticides, so it is important to wash them thoroughly or buy organic ones.

Cherries
These small fruits stimulate and cleanse the body and remove toxins from the kidneys, liver and digestive system. They also contain betacarotene, vitamin C, B vitamins and potassium. The darker the cherry, the better.

Mangoes
Naturopaths believe that these fragrant fruits can cleanse the blood and benefit the kidneys and digestion. Mangoes provide rich amounts of vitamin C, betacarotene and potassium.

Papayas
Also known as pawpaws, papayas contain an enzyme called papain, which helps the digestion of protein and benefits the digestive system. However, levels of this enzyme diminish the more the fruit ripens. Papaya's supplies of betacarotene and vitamin C can benefit the skin, hair and nails. Calcium, iron and potassium are also present.

Melons
These aromatic, fleshy fruits have a high water content and are an effective diuretic and kidney cleanser. If eaten on their own or with other fruit, melons are easy to digest and pass quickly through the system, which is why they are so often served as a starter. Orange-fleshed melons, such as cantaloupe and Charentais are particularly rich in betacarotene and vitamin C.

Pineapples
Rich in betacarotene, vitamin C and folic acid, pineapples also contain the antibacterial enzyme bromelain, which aids the digestion of protein and has anti-inflammatory qualities. Bromelain is destroyed if pineapples are canned. Calcium, potassium and magnesium are also present.

JUICING
Fresh fruit and vegetable juices have a powerful effect on the body, stimulating the whole system and encouraging the elimination of toxins. They play a vital role in detoxing and should be drunk fresh. Processing reduces their nutritional content so cartons or bottles of juice should be avoided.

As a rule, fruit juices should be drunk in the morning because they have a stronger detoxifying effect than vegetable juices. They scour waste products from the gastro-intestinal tract and have a mild laxative effect. Vegetable juices are best taken later in the day. They are useful for re-establishing the acid and alkaline balance of the body and also help to rejuvenate.

When making juices at home, choose ripe fruits, which contain higher levels of nutrients, but avoid any that look old or soft. Fresh juices can be very strong, so dilute with filtered or mineral water. They should always be drunk as soon as they are made because vitamin levels soon begin to diminish.

Juice Benefits
• Fresh juices are easy to digest and flush out the digestive system.
• They are believed to speed up the metabolism, cleanse the blood and strengthen the immune system.
• Antioxidant vitamins found in fresh juices help to fight illness and curb the signs of aging.
• Juices enhance our vitality and improve energy levels.
• The enzymes and amino acids found in juices stimulate the cleansing process and speed up the absorption of enzymes in the body.

Note: Fresh juices should be avoided if you suffer from candida, diabetes or bowel disorders.

DRIED FRUIT
This is a useful addition to a detox programme. Higher in calories than fresh fruit, dried fruit provides plenty of sustaining energy and is an invaluable pick-me-up during a detox. Unlike other high sugar foods, such as chocolate and confectionery, dried fruit is a good source of nutrients.

Look for unsulphured fruit, especially if you suffer from asthma. Dried hunza apricots are delicious, as are dried figs, dates, raisins, apples, peaches and mangoes.

VEGETABLES

These are the mainstay of any detox or healthy eating plan. They are packed with vitamins, minerals, bioflavonoids and other phytochemicals, and offer an abundance of therapeutic benefits. While fruits are generally powerful cleansers, vegetables are known for their calming effect on the body, balancing acid and alkaline levels and providing sustenance.

Carrots

These orange root vegetables offer a huge range of benefits and are one of the best detoxifiers. Carrots are reputed to cleanse, nourish and stimulate the whole body, particularly the liver, kidneys and digestive system. Their rich supply of betacarotene has been found to lower the risk of cancer. According to a recent study, eating just one medium-size carrot a day could reduce the risk of lung cancer by half, even among ex-smokers. For the greatest benefits, consume your daily quota of carrot nutrients as fresh juice.

Beetroot

This vibrantly coloured, ruby-red vegetable is thought to be one of the best liver cleansers. It is an effective detoxifier and laxative, and has long been considered beneficial to the blood. Beetroot is best eaten raw, when levels of betacarotene, vitamin C, calcium and iron are at their highest.

Onions and garlic

These vegetables and their relations, leeks, are rich in antiviral and antibacterial nutrients, which are reputed to cleanse the system. They are said to be the richest dietary source of quercetin, a potent antioxidant, which has been shown to fight cancer and lower blood cholesterol. Onions are at their most potent when they are eaten raw but, unlike most other vegetables, their healing properties are not all lost when the vegetable is cooked.

Garlic is one of the most potent healers. It boosts the immune system, acts as an anti-inflammatory and is said to help lift the spirits.

Cabbage

To gain the greatest health benefits from cabbage, it should be eaten raw or juiced. In this form, it is particularly potent and is rich in antiviral and antibacterial nutrients. Cabbage contains betacarotene, vitamins C and E, folate, potassium, thiamin and iron. It aids the digestion, detoxifies the stomach and upper bowels and cleanses the liver. The famous German cabbage dish, sauerkraut, is said to be excellent for improving digestion and levels of intestinal flora.

Broccoli

This vegetable is a member of the cruciferous family, which also includes cabbage, cauliflower, watercress, Brussels sprouts, greens and swede, and is definitely one of the detox superfoods. It stimulates the liver and supplies the body with a powerful combination of phytochemicals. These provide a cancer-fighting cocktail that plays a crucial role in fighting disease by stimulating the body's enzyme defences. Broccoli also provides many of the B vitamins and a good supply of vitamin C, calcium, folate, iron, potassium and zinc.

Above: Garlic boasts antiviral, antibacterial and antifungal qualities and is believed to be one of the top cancer-fighting foods.

Above: Tomatoes are believed to stimulate the liver, which plays a key role in eliminating harmful toxins from the body.

Tomatoes
These fleshy vegetables are reputed to stimulate the liver and reduce inflammation caused by hepatitis and cirrhosis. Tomatoes are at their nutritional peak when served raw or juiced.

Choose organic, vine-ripened fruit to avoid unwanted pesticides and ensure higher levels of vitamin C and E, betacarotene, calcium, magnesium and phosphorus. Levels of these nutrients are much lower in tomatoes that are picked when they are green, and they decline significantly when tomatoes are cooked or canned.

Tomatoes are a common allergen, and can trigger skin rashes as well as exacerbate the symptoms of arthritis.

Spinach
This leafy vegetable is an excellent source of antioxidant nutrients and is best eaten raw. It contains about four times more betacarotene than broccoli, as well as containing a rich supply of vitamin C. Spinach also contains calcium, folate, iron, potassium, thiamin and zinc, although the quantities of iron are not as high as once thought. Spinach contains oxalic acid, which inhibits the absorption of calcium and iron. However, eating spinach with a vitamin C-rich food will improve iron absorption.

Fennel
This is known to be an effective diuretic and has a calming effect on the stomach. It contains useful amounts of betacarotene and folate.

Celery
A recognized diuretic and laxative, celery plays a vital part in any detox programme. In natural medicine, celery juice is prescribed as a sedative and is even said to boost the sex drive.

Watercress
This invigorating and stimulating green leafy vegetable is part of the cruciferous family and shares the cancer-fighting properties of that group. It is reputed to be effective for cleansing the blood and is particularly good for improving the condition of the skin.

Cucumber
Although this vegetable does not have a particularly high nutritional content, it is possibly the most effective diuretic in the vegetable world. It helps to improve the efficiency of the kidneys, as well as assisting with the elimination of waste and preventing water retention. Cucumber also aids the digestion and soothes the system.

Above: Cucumber is an excellent diuretic and is said to stimulate the kidneys.

Lettuce
Although lettuce and other salad leaves contain about 90 per cent water, they supply useful amounts of nutrients. Antioxidant betacarotene, vitamin C, folate and iron are all present. Levels of these nutrients will vary depending on the type of leaf and the freshness of the lettuce but, generally, the darker, outer leaves are more nutritious than the paler ones that are found towards the centre of the vegetable. In natural medicine, lettuce is often prescribed for its calming, sedative properties and is recommended to soothe the nerves and aid sleep.

BUY ORGANIC
The aim of detoxing is to eliminate unwanted toxins from the body, so it makes sense to avoid foods that contain pesticides and additives, and buy organic foods instead. Organic fruit and vegetables may be more expensive but, if you can afford it, the health benefits – and often the taste – are well worth the extra cost. It is important to wash non-organic fruit and vegetables thoroughly or peel them before eating. Remember also to scrub the skins of citrus fruits thoroughly as they can sometimes be treated with a wax preservative.

GRAINS

Wholegrains and cereals are a vital part of a cleansing, healthy diet. They are an excellent low-fat source of protein, complex carbohydrates, fibre, vitamins and minerals and, in addition, are inexpensive, readily available and increadibly versatile. Grains have been cultivated for centuries and formed a major part of our ancestor's diets.

Look for wholegrains that are largely unprocessed, as they retain most of their nutrients as well as soluble and insoluble fibre. Both types of fibre are fundamental to good health and prevent constipation, colon and rectal cancers, ulcers, heart disease and diverticulitis. Eating foods rich in soluble fibre has been shown to reduce harmful levels of cholesterol in the blood. The fibre binds with cholesterol, helping it to pass through, and be eliminated from, the body. Insoluble fibre helps to speed up the passage and digestion of food through the intestines.

Grains to include in your detox programme include: brown rice, barley, millet, couscous, oats, corn, buckwheat and quinoa. The starch present in wholegrains is absorbed slowly, keeping blood sugar levels on an even keel, which is important during a detox when you may be eating less than your body is used to. Brown rice is also said to treat digestive disorders, calm the nervous system, prevent kidney stones and reduce the risk of bowel cancer.

Note: Wheat should be avoided during a detox programme. Although this grain is nutritionally valuable in its whole form, it is also a common allergen. It can irritate the digestive system and can also inhibit the body's ability to absorb some nutrients.

Below: Unprocessed wholegrains provide a valuable supply of fibre, which helps to eliminate toxins from the body and reduce harmful levels of cholesterol.

SUPER FOODS

There are certain foods that are particularly effective at stimulating the elimination of toxins:

Wheatgrass is a powerful detoxifier when juiced. As well as being a rich source of vitamins A, C and E, B vitamins and all known minerals, it contains chlorophyll, which works directly on the liver to eliminate toxins. Barleygrass has similar properties to wheatgrass.

Spirulina is a powerful antioxidant and contains betacarotene, B vitamins and iron. It works on the lymphatic system and strengthens the body's defences.

Chlorella is a powerful antioxidant, blood tonic and cleanser. It contains a high concentration of chlorophyll and is a good source of fibre, both of which stimulate the cleansing of the bowel.

Aloe vera helps to balance the gastro-intestinal system, helping digestion and easing irritable bowel syndrome and constipation.

Psyllium husks are the seeds of the plantain. They provide rich amounts of natural fibre, which is good for cleansing the colon. Linseeds have the same effect.

Above: (clockwise from top) Chlorella, spirulina, aloe vera, psyllium and wheatgrass will enhance a detox.

Left: Beans and pulses produce a slow rise in blood sugar, ensuring sustained long-term energy, which is vital during a detox.

SEA VEGETABLES

The West has only recently acknowledged the remarkable health benefits of sea vegetables, which have been an essential part of the Asian diet for centuries. They are one of nature's superfoods, packed with vital nutrients, including antioxidant betacarotene and certain B vitamins, calcium, iron, magnesium, phosphorus and potassium, along with trace elements, such as selenium, zinc and iodine. This rich balance of minerals benefits the nervous system and boosts the immune system and metabolism. Research shows that alginic acid, found in some seaweeds such as kombu, arame, hijiki and wakame, binds with heavy metals, such as cadmium, lead, mercury and radium, in the intestines, successfully eliminating them from the body. Sea vegetables also improve the condition of the skin, hair and nails. There is a wide range to choose from with lava, arame and kombu being the most popular. Sea vegetables are delicious in sushi, sprinkled over salads or in soups.

BEANS AND PULSES

These are a vital part of a cleansing diet. They provide plenty of low-fat protein, fibre, vitamins and minerals, including folate, iron, magnesium, manganese, phosphorus and potassium. The high fibre content helps to relieve constipation and lowers levels of blood cholesterol, reducing the risk of heart disease and stroke. Studies show that eating half a cup of cooked beans on a regular basis can reduce cholesterol levels by almost 20 per cent. Beans also contain phytoestrogens, which are reputed to balance hormone levels and protect against certain cancers. Lentils, soya beans, dried peas and chick-peas are particularly nutritious.

It is possible to find organic beans that are canned in water, but most canned beans have salt and sugar added to them during processing, making it preferable to use dried beans. Most dried beans need to be soaked for at least eight hours before cooking. They should then be boiled hard for at least 10 minutes, before reducing the heat to a simmer.

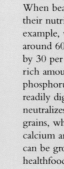

SUPERSPROUTS

When beans, seeds and grains sprout, their nutritional content soars. For example, vitamin C increases by around 60 per cent and B vitamins by 30 per cent. Sprouts also supply rich amounts of protein, vitamin E, phosphorus and potassium in a readily digestible form. Sprouting neutralizes the phytates found in grains, which are believed to impair calcium and zinc absorption. Sprouts can be grown at home or found in healthfood shops and supermarkets.

Above: Lava and arame boost the immune system and metabolism.

NUTS AND SEEDS

An excellent protein-packed alternative to meat and cheese, nuts are said to reduce the risk of heart disease, stroke and certain cancers and to improve the skin, hair and nails. They are packed with vitamin E, B vitamins, calcium, iron, magnesium, phosphorus, potassium and essential fatty acids. Walnuts, almonds, cashews, hazelnuts and chestnuts offer some of the best health benefits.

Nuts have a high fat content, so should be eaten in moderation and salted types should be avoided.

Seeds, such as pumpkin, sesame, sunflower and linseeds, offer huge health benefits. Rich in the antioxidant vitamin E, they support the immune

Above: Nuts and seeds are packed with health-giving properties.

system, protecting cells from oxidation. Vitamin E improves the circulation and works in tandem with betacarotene and vitamin C to reduce the risk of certain cancers and heart disease. Seeds, in particular sunflower seeds, contain omega-6 fatty acids, which are known to reduce blood cholesterol levels. Seeds are delicious sprinkled over stir-fries, soups, salads and stews.

Note: Nuts and seeds are prone to rancidity, which hinders any health benefits. Buy them in small quantities and store in airtight containers in a dark, cool place.

GET THE MOST FROM YOUR FOOD

Buy fruit, vegetables, nuts, grains, seeds and beans from a reputable retailer with a regular turnover of stock to ensure optimum freshness.

Do not buy fresh produce from street markets that are located near busy, polluted roads. Also try to avoid buying fresh produce that is displayed under fluorescent lighting as this can set off a harmful chemical reaction that depletes their nutrient content.

Loose, fresh produce is much easier to check for quality than prepacked, and both fresh and packaged goods should be bought in small amounts to avoid prolonged storage.

Avoid peeling fresh organic produce whenever possible, and do not prepare too far in advance as nutrients, such as vitamin C, will be destroyed.

Finally, remember that fruit and vegetables are at their most nutritious and are easiest to digest when raw. Steaming and baking are preferable options when cooking.

HERBS

Although herbs generally have a low nutritional value, they are highly revered for their therapeutic qualities. Their restorative powers are due to the high concentration of essential oils, which are antioxidant, antiviral and antibacterial. Most herbs have a calming, cleansing effect on the digestive system, easing constipation, nausea and stomach cramps, improving the circulation and relieving indigestion, headaches and respiratory problems. Some of the most useful herbs for cooking are basil, coriander, dill, mint, parsley and rosemary, sage and thyme.

Herbs can also be enjoyed in teas and infusions. They make a healthy alternative to tea and coffee and are

SUPER HERBS

There are a number of herbal remedies available in health food shops that can complement your detox by stimulating the body's cleansing processes. Consult a qualified naturopath or practitioner before taking any of them.

Milk thistle increases the efficiency of the liver and its ability to filter out toxins. It is also said to relieve hangovers.

Echinacea boosts the immune system and fights harmful bacteria.

Dandelion leaf and root are effective digestives, as well as liver and gall bladder tonics.

Gotu kola has been shown to diminish cellulite.

Goldenseal is a digestive and an antibacterial herb.

Ginger root cleanses and rejuvenates the digestive system.

Above: Enjoy the calming properties of fresh herbs, such as coriander, mint and parsley, in salads, cooked dishes and infusions.

easy and economical to make at home. Place 10ml/2 tsp of fresh leaves in a jug and pour over boiling water. Cover and leave for about 10 minutes to infuse, then strain into a cup or heatproof glass. Peppermint tea assists digestion while camomile tea has a calming, sedative effect and is best taken before bedtime to aid sleep.

SPICES

These have been revered for their medicinal and culinary properties for thousands of years. When eaten, spices tend to have a stimulating, toning and antiseptic effect on the body.

One of the most powerful healing spices that should be included in the diet is fresh root ginger. It can treat gastro-intestinal disorders and nausea, and can reduce the risk of certain cancers. Useful spices to include in a detox programme are fenugreek, nutmeg and turmeric, because of their ability to cleanse the body and aid the release of toxins. Other healing spices are cardamom, which calms indigestion; cinnamon, which is an effective detoxifier and cleanser; cloves, which have antiseptic and anaesthetic qualities; and coriander, which relieves nausea and diarrhoea.

OILS AND VINEGARS

Oils have an important role to play when detoxing, yet choosing the right type of fat and using it in moderate amounts is vital. Stick to oils, such as extra virgin and virgin olive oils, and unrefined, cold-pressed oils, including safflower, sunflower and rapeseed oil, as they provide essential fatty acids as well as vitamin E. Oils are prone to rancidity and, with the exception of olive oil, can become unstable when heated. Always store oils in a dark, cool place and buy in small quantities to ensure freshness.

Speciality oils, such as walnut, almond, sesame and hazelnut, also contain valuable essential fatty acids. They supply a great deal of flavour when sprinkled in small quantities over salads and stir-fried dishes.

Wine vinegars should generally be avoided when detoxing as they contain acetic acid, which hinders digestion and prevents the assimilation of foods. Cider vinegar, however, is favoured for its many health-giving properties. It is also believed to relieve the symptoms of arthritis and headaches.

Above: Fresh root ginger, fenugreek and coriander seeds are all powerful detox spices, which work to cleanse and tone the system.

DETOX VEGETABLE STOCK

Vegetable stock is often used to add extra flavour to dishes like stews and soups. However, shop-bought stocks are often very high in salt and should not be used when detoxing. It is easy to make your own stock at home, using fresh, organic ingredients. It can be frozen or stored in the fridge for up to four days so, if you are planning to use it for recipes during your detox, make a batch as part of your detox preparations.

To make a detox vegetable stock, heat 15ml/1 tbsp sunflower oil in a large saucepan. Add 1 chopped potato, 1 chopped carrot, 1 chopped onion and 1 chopped celery stick and cook, covered, for 10 minutes or until softened. Stir in 2 peeled garlic cloves, 1 sprig of thyme, 1 bay leaf and a few stalks of parsley. Pour 600ml/1 pint/ 2½ cups water into the pan and bring to the boil, then simmer, partially covered, for 40 minutes. Strain, season with freshly ground black pepper and use as required.

BODY AND MIND

Although making changes to your diet is the most effective way of eliminating toxins, complementary therapies, exercise and relaxation techniques can also prove to be helpful. A detox will be more effective and more fun if you include some of the exercises and therapies below.

EXERCISING YOUR BODY

Not only does exercise tone the muscles, it also lifts the spirits, energizing both body and mind. Exercise is a valuable part of a detox as it stimulates the lymphatic system and gets the heart going. It also improves circulation – efficiently transporting oxygen and nutrients to cells while removing waste.

Aerobic exercise is one of the most effective ways of stimulating the system. It is recommended that you do 20–30 minutes of swimming, cycling or jogging, or take an exercise class three times a week. Simple stretch movements will also stimulate the circulation and tone the body.

Exercise encourages the release of endorphins, which induce a feeling of heightened mental awareness. However, avoid over-exercising or doing anything too strenuous during a detox as your energy levels are likely to be lower than normal. Conversely, do not become a couch potato.

The following forms of exercise are excellent during a detox:

- Yoga
- Exercise classes
- Pilates
- Swimming
- Brisk walking
- Cycling
- Stretching
- Low-impact aerobics
- Dancing
- T'ai chi

EXERCISING YOUR MIND

Relaxation, de-stressing and clearing the mind of negativity are just as important as physical exercise and diet during a detox. Body and mind are fully integrated, and stress, anger, fear and negative thoughts can be damaging to the system, reducing its ability to eliminate toxins. Stress can wear you down, making you more susceptible to infections and disease. As well as poor health, stress will make you tired,

depressed, irritable and affect your concentration. In a stressful situation, the body produces adrenaline, which induces a "ready-for-action" state in the body. When there is no outlet for this, it can affect our internal organs, manifesting itself as a headache or causing tense shoulders, indigestion or skin problems. Deep relaxation will benefit not just your mental state, but your body too. Some of the following could help you relax:

- Learn how to meditate. Just five minutes a day can reduce tension, increase concentration and help relieve stress-related conditions.

Above: Meditation is excellent for reducing stress levels and improving concentration.

- Put on some calming music and sit back with a good book.
- Try a simple breathing exercise: breathe in, tensing your shoulders, arms and hands. Hold for a few seconds, then breathe out, letting it all go – repeat 3–4 times.
- Try some gentle stretching exercises or a yoga, t'ai chi or Pilates class.
- Focus on your breathing. Breathe slowly and deeply from your stomach.
- Have a massage, facial, manicure or pedicure.

USING VISUALIZATION

This is a very simple and effective relaxation technique.
1 Lie down in a quiet place and close your eyes. Try to clear your mind and relax your muscles.
2 Imagine yourself in an idyllic, peaceful place, where you feel completely comfortable and safe, such as a sandy beach or the countryside. Use all your senses to visualize the colours, smells, sounds, feel and taste.
3 Think of a short and positive statement, such as "I am calm and relaxed" and repeat it a few times. You can escape to your favourite place whenever you feel stressed.

COMPLEMENTARY THERAPIES

Therapies such as massage, reflexology, shiatsu and acupressure are not just relaxing, they offer great therapeutic benefits too. Massage stimulates the lymphatic system and boosts circulation, helping to eliminate toxins.

Reflexology massages the acupressure points on the feet, and sometimes the hands and ears, and has been shown to help to rebalance the body. Shiatsu and acupressure are based on similar principles to those of reflexology but incorporate the whole body and, in the case of shiatsu, can also involve stretching and manipulation.

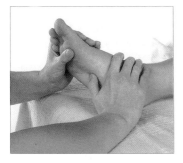

Above: A skilled reflexologist can treat the whole of your body through your feet.

HYDROTHERAPY

Water therapy is not only relaxing but boosts the circulation, opens and unblocks the pores and encourages the removal of toxins.

Aromatherapy bath

Run a warm bath and add a few drops of essential oil. Choose relaxing oils that you instantly like the smell of. Calming oils include camomile, lavender, sandalwood, myrrh, frankincense and patchouli. Stimulating oils, which are also rebalancing and diuretic, include rosemary, geranium and rose.

Epsom salts bath

These encourage the elimination of toxins through your skin. The salts are high in magnesium, which is good for tired muscles. Pour 450g/1lb Epsom salts into a warm bath and lie back for 20 minutes, adding more hot water if the bath becomes too cool. Afterwards, pat yourself dry, wrap yourself in a warm towel and go to bed or relax for an hour. You may sweat during the night, so drink plenty of water before you retire. In the morning, have a bath or shower to remove any salty residues.

Sitz bath

Spend a few minutes in a warm bath, then have a very brief icy-cold shower or bath. The temperature change stimulates the circulation and internal organs, encouraging removal of toxins.

Sauna and steam bath

These encourage perspiration and boost the circulation, which aids the removal of toxins. Spend 5–10 minutes in the sauna or steam room at a time, taking a cold shower or swim in between. Finish with a cold shower. Relax for 30 minutes to allow your body to adjust to normal temperature.

Note: If you suffer from heart problems, avoid any of these baths. If you suffer from eczema or high blood pressure, avoid the Epsom salts bath.

Above: It is worth investing in a range of essential oils for adding to your bath water.

SKIN BRUSHING

Dry skin brushing, using a natural bristle brush, is a wonderfully exhilarating way of boosting your circulation. It makes your skin smooth and soft and helps with the elimination of cellulite, because it encourages the lymphatic system and the expulsion of toxins through the skin. The whole process should take less than 10 minutes and it is a great way to wake up in the morning before taking a bath or shower. It also increases the effectiveness of an aromatherapy bath.
1 Start at your feet and toes, brushing up the front and back of your legs using long strokes (always brush towards your heart). Move up to your thighs and groin area.
2 Brush over your buttocks, up to the lower back.
3 Now brush your hands and arms, moving towards the heart, using long, smooth strokes.
4 Brush your stomach using circular, clockwise movements. This will stimulate the colon.
5 Move across your shoulders, down over your chest, then down your back, towards your heart.

HOW TO DETOX

Following a detox should be a positive, relaxing and rejuvenating experience, so it is essential that you are in a positive, stress-free state of mind. Before embarking on a detox programme, you should be fully prepared as this is the key to a successful detox. Even if you are just following the one-day plan, it is vital to familiarize yourself with the detox plan to reap the full benefits.

PREPARING FOR A DETOX
There is no right or wrong time of the year to detox, but certain times – such as the start of spring, summer or autumn – are best. If you want to detox in the winter, it may be a good idea to include more lightly cooked, steamed or baked foods, especially if you are following the seven-day or two-week detox plans.

Check your diary and choose a time when you know you can take time to relax and sleep. Let your friends and family know about your plans to embark on a detox. This will avoid unwanted phone calls and surprise visits. You might like to book a massage or practise some massage techniques. This is also a perfect time to treat yourself to some good-quality aromatherapy oils, perfumed candles, incense sticks, new tapes and CDs, books and magazines.

Stock up on everything you need for a one-day or weekend detox to avoid endless trips to the supermarket during the detox itself. If you are embarking on a longer plan, you will have to stock up on fresh produce during the detox.

Ensure your surroundings are clean and tidy so that you do not have to think about tidying up when on the detox. Remove clutter, piles of old papers, and empty the bins.

A day or two before starting a detox programme, begin to prepare yourself. Eat simple, fresh foods and cut down on meat and dairy products, alcohol, wheat, sugary food, tea and coffee, junk food and cigarettes – or, if you can, cut them out completely. This will ease your body into the detox. If you want to detox for longer than two weeks, seek professional advice.

Above: Fresh, raw organic fruit and vegetables are the keystones of a successful detox, encouraging the elimination of toxins and giving your system a well-earned rest.

SIDE-EFFECTS OF A DETOX
You may well experience side-effects when following a detox programme. These will depend on how toxic you are and the length of the detox programme that you choose. These side-effects are known as a "cleansing crisis" and are a result of the body trying to cope with the influx of toxins that have been released into the system from the fat cells, where they were previously stored. Don't feel alarmed by your body reacting in this way. It is perfectly normal.

Side-effects can include tiredness, headaches, nausea, feeling cold, bad breath or a furry tongue, constipation, diarrhoea and irritability. Don't let this put you off. Experiencing side-effects can actually be a positive sign and indicates that your body is beginning to eliminate toxins. If you do experience unpleasant side-effects, it is important to avoid taking painkillers, as these can be detrimental to detoxing. The symptoms will pass quickly but, in the meantime, drink plenty of water and herbal teas, make sure you get plenty of rest, and try to think about the benefits that will be gained from your detox.

Weight loss is also likely because of the restrictive nature of a detox diet and may be beneficial if you are overweight. However, it is important to remember that this is not the underlying purpose of a detox.

WHEN NOT TO DETOX
As long as you are fit and healthy, there is no reason why you should not embark on a detox. However, if you have any concerns about the impact a detox may have on your health, consult a doctor first. Do not start a detox programme in any of the following circumstances:
• Directly after a bout of flu, a cold or food poisoning.
• If you are under a lot of pressure at work, have just moved house or are feeling emotionally vulnerable. Wait for a time when your life is slightly calmer.
• If you are taking prescription drugs, have any serious medical conditions, have liver disease or have suffered kidney failure.
• If you are pregnant, breastfeeding or diabetic.
• If you are recovering from alcohol or drug addiction. It is important to seek medical advice before detoxing.

THE ONE-DAY MONO DIET

A one-day mono diet is an excellent introduction to detoxing and is based on eating just one type of raw fruit or vegetable for a whole day. You are unlikely to feel any dramatic side-effects but a mono-diet will have a noticeable positive effect on your health and general well-being.

A one-day mono diet will give your digestive system a rest, allowing it to concentrate on eliminating stored toxins. Rather than eating three meals in a day, you can eat more frequently throughout the day but only small amounts of your chosen fruit or vegetable at a time. Raw fruit and vegetables have a powerful cleansing effect on the body and also supply plenty of vitamins, minerals and fibre. If you can, choose a day when you are not working and take time to rest, relax and sleep. You will benefit more by taking this time out to devote yourself fully to the detox.

FRUIT AND VEGETABLES
Choose just *one* of the fruits or vegetables in the list below as your food for the day.
• Grapes
• Apples
• Pears
• Pineapple
• Papaya
• Carrots
• Cucumber
• Celery

Above: Although a mono diet restricts you to just one type of fruit or vegetable, you can choose a variety of ways to prepare it.

SHOPPING
It is best to choose organic fruit and vegetables for a detox as they do not contain toxic pesticides. You will need:
• 1–1.5kg/2–3lb of your chosen fruit or vegetable
• 2 litres/3½ pints/8 cups still mineral water (or drink filtered water instead)
• herbal teas or fresh herbs to infuse

TWO DAYS BEFORE
Prepare for your detox by cutting down on meat and dairy products, salt, wheat, tea and coffee, and sugary foods. Avoid alcohol and cigarettes.

THE DAY BEFORE
The evening before your mono diet, eat a light evening meal. A vegetable and bean soup or a stir-fry would be perfect. Have an aromatherapy bath to relax and go to bed early with a good book and unwind.

DETOX DAY
Morning Start your day with a cup of hot water, flavoured with the juice of half a lemon. This will give a kick-start to the liver. Do some simple stretching exercises to stimulate your lymphatic system. Run a bath and, while it is running, give yourself a dry skin brush to stimulate your circulation. For breakfast, prepare your chosen fruit or vegetable. Sip water at regular intervals throughout the day.

Late morning Have a massage or shiatsu, reflexology or acupressure session, or try some relaxation techniques. Eat some of your fruit or vegetable and drink plenty of water.

Lunch For lunch, prepare your fruit or vegetable, but perhaps try it in a different guise, such as grated, chopped or juiced. Drink plenty of water.

Above: A substantial bean soup makes a good meal the evening before your detox.

Afternoon Try doing some gentle exercises, such as yoga, Pilates or body-conditioning, or do some brisk walking, cycling or swimming. Follow this exercise with some of your fruit or vegetable and a herbal tea.

Evening Finish your quota of fruit or vegetable. Meditate or practise a relaxation technique, such as visualization. Pamper yourself with a manicure or pedicure, watch TV or read a book and listen to some calming music. Have an Epsom salts bath, then retreat to bed early.

THE DAY AFTER DETOXING
It is important to ease your body out of a detox gradually. Over the next few days, return to a healthy, varied diet based on the key cleansing foods and the recipes in this book. Start your day as you did during the detox by drinking a cup of hot water and lemon juice, followed by some simple stretching exercises. Try not to over-exert yourself and, if possible, avoid subjecting yourself to stressful situations that may cause anxiety.

THE WEEKEND DETOX

This two-day detox programme is based on fruit and vegetable dishes and juices. It is a gentle but effective detox that will provide your digestive system with a rest, allowing it to concentrate on eliminating toxins. You will probably feel some side-effects, but these are perfectly normal.

For this diet choose a weekend when you are not too busy and allow yourself plenty of time to rest and relax. Book a massage or complementary therapy and take some gentle exercise, such as a brisk walk, to stimulate the circulation and metabolism. Choose cleansing fruit-based juices in the morning and re-juvenating vegetable-based juices later in the day. Drink plenty of water throughout the weekend.

TWO DAYS BEFORE

Follow the guidelines given for two days before the one-day mono diet.

Above: Couscous with Vegetables makes an ideal light meal the evening before starting a detox because it provides plenty of sustained long-term energy.

THE DAY BEFORE

The evening before your weekend detox, have a light, vegetable-based meal. Choose one of the soups, salads or cleansing meals from the recipe section and follow with one of the healthy desserts. Unwind in a soothing aromatherapy bath and go to bed early to read and relax.

Above: Start the day with a fruit-based juice to kick-start the cleansing process.

DAY ONE

Morning When you wake up, drink a cup of hot water, flavoured with the juice of half a lemon. This will give a kick-start to the liver. If you like, return to bed and relax. Do some simple stretching exercises to stimulate your lymphatic system. Run a bath, giving yourself a dry skin brush to stimulate your circulation while it runs. For breakfast, prepare a fruit juice from the recipe section, diluting with water.

Late morning Have a massage or shiatsu, reflexology or acupressure session, or try a relaxation technique. Eat some fruit, such as an apple, a pear or some grapes, and drink a herbal tea. Go for a walk before lunchtime.

Lunch Choose a vegetable juice from the recipe section and make a large salad with tomatoes, cucumber, fennel, carrot, and beetroot, and a dressing of olive oil, garlic and lemon juice.

Afternoon Relax after lunch. Try some gentle exercise, such as yoga, Pilates, stretching, walking, cycling or swimming. Drink plenty of water.

Teatime Choose a vegetable-based juice from the recipe section.

Evening Between 6 and 8 pm, have an evening meal of lightly steamed vegetables, sprinkled with fresh herbs and lemon juice, accompanied by organic brown rice. Alternatively, make a vegetable stir-fry or a large salad. Meditate or practise a relaxation technique, such as visualization. Have an Epsom salts bath and retire to bed early, drinking plenty of water before you go to sleep.

DAY TWO

Take it easy as you may feel tired today. Repeat the same routine followed on day one, but choose different fruit and vegetable juices. In the morning, brush your skin and take a sitz bath. In the afternoon, try having a sauna or steam, followed by a swim.

Note: Do not have an Epsom salts bath today.

THE DAY AFTER DETOXING

Follow the recommendations given for the one-day mono diet.

Above: Beansprouts are full of nutrients and are excellent cleansers, making them the perfect ingredient in a detox stir-fry.

THE SEVEN-DAY DETOX

This is a more rigorous diet plan but it is still designed to provide a slow and gentle detox. The programme combines and supplements the one-day mono diet and weekend detox plan and is extremely effective in cleansing and revitalizing the whole system.

It is not essential to take a week off work to follow this slightly longer programme. However, if you cannot take time off, it is recommended that you start the detox on a Friday, as the first few days are more intense. This will give you time to rest over the weekend. Have a maximum of two Epsom salts baths during this detox.

TWO DAYS BEFORE
Follow the guidelines given for two days before the one-day mono diet.

Above: Broccoli and garlic make a cleansing combination for a light detox meal.

THE DAY BEFORE
Follow the guidelines given for the day before the weekend detox.

DAY ONE
Follow the detox guidelines given for the one-day mono diet.

DAYS TWO AND THREE
Follow the detox guidelines given for the weekend detox. In the evening, have an aromatherapy or sitz bath.

DAYS FOUR AND FIVE
Morning Repeat the same routine followed on days two and three, and include a fruit salad made of three types of fruit with a spoonful of yogurt.

Late morning Eat some fruit, such as an apple or grapes, and drink a herbal tea. Go for a gentle walk before lunch.

Lunch Eat a large leafy salad, sprinkled with sunflower seeds and a little dressing made from olive oil and lemon juice.

Afternoon Have a rest after lunch. If you can, do some gentle exercises, such as yoga, Pilates, stretching, body-conditioning, swimming, cycling or walking. Drink a cup of herbal tea.

Teatime Choose a vegetable juice from the recipe section. Alternatively, have a snack of vegetable crudités or a handful of mixed sunflower and pumpkin seeds.

Evening For your evening meal, eat one of the following: a baked potato topped with steamed or stir-fried vegetables, sprinkled with lemon juice and sesame seeds; steamed or stir-fried vegetables with organic brown rice or buckwheat noodles and tofu; a large mixed salad with tofu, and a dressing made from sunflower oil, toasted sesame oil, crushed garlic, lemon juice and sesame seeds; or a large salad with a baked potato, topped with a spoonful of Hummus (see recipe section).

HEALTHY SNACKS
From day four, you can introduce some snacks if you are feeling peckish or are lacking in energy. Try some of the following:
• Sunflower or pumpkin seeds
• Fruit or vegetable crudités
• Rice cakes
• Dried fruit
• Non-wheat crackers

Above: Tomato and Lentil Dahl is a nutritious mix of vegetables and pulses.

DAYS SIX AND SEVEN
Morning and late morning Repeat the same routine followed on days four and five but have a bowl of dried fruit stewed with fresh root ginger.

Lunch Choose one of the following from the recipe section: a large salad with a spoonful of Hummus; Pea Guacamole with Crudités and rice cakes; Warm Vegetable Salad with a baked potato; Japanese Salad; Date, Orange and Carrot Salad. For dessert, have a bowl of live natural yogurt with a spoonful of organic honey.

Teatime Repeat the same routine followed on days four and five.

Evening For your evening meal make one of the following recipes: Roasted Root Vegetable Soup; Fresh Cabbage Soup with a large grain or bean salad; Tomato and Lentil Dahl; Couscous with Vegetables; or Brown Rice Risotto with Mushrooms. Take a second Epsom salts bath.

THE DAY AFTER DETOXING
Follow the recommendations given for the one-day mono diet.

THE TWO-WEEK LIVER-CLEANSING DIET

Optimum health depends on the efficiency of the liver, which is responsible for over 500 functions. If the liver becomes overloaded, harmful substances are stored in it, as well as in the fat cells around the body. Symptoms of an unhappy liver range from headaches, cellulite, irritable bowel syndrome, poor digestion, bloating, depression and mood changes, to the more serious problems of diabetes, hepatitis and cirrhosis. Reassuringly, the liver has an incredible capacity to regenerate itself – even after many years of neglect – and it can really benefit from a tailor-made cleansing detox.

Above: Fresh fruit and vegetable juices stimulate and cleanse the whole system.

HOW TO MAINTAIN HEALTHY LIVER FUNCTION

- Drink eight glasses of water a day.
- Include plenty of fresh fruit and vegetables as well as wholegrains, nuts, seeds and beans in your diet.
- Avoid foods to which you may be allergic or intolerant.
- Eat organic foods whenever possible.
- Avoid overcooked, processed, fried, sugary and junk foods.
- Keep your consumption of alcohol and caffeine to a minimum.
- Exercise regularly.
- Try taking a supplement that can support the liver and encourage the removal of toxins.

LIVER-CLEANSING FOODS

The following can benefit the liver: apples, alfalfa sprouts, artichokes, asparagus, garlic, beetroot, broccoli, cabbage, carrots, fresh root ginger, green leafy vegetables and bitter leaves, such as dandelion.

TWO DAYS BEFORE

Follow the guidelines given for two days before the one-day mono diet.

THE DAY BEFORE

Follow the guidelines given for the day before the weekend detox.

DAY ONE

Follow the detox guidelines given for the one-day mono diet.

DAYS TWO AND THREE

The programme for these two days is based on fruit and vegetable juices as well as salads, lightly cooked vegetables and brown rice. Start by following the detox guidelines given for the weekend detox.

On day three you may feel tired and lacking in energy, so take it easy. Try having a sauna or a steam, followed by a swim in the afternoon, if you feel like it. In the evening, take an aromatherapy bath to relax and go to bed early with a book.

Morning When you wake up, drink a cup of hot water, with the juice of half a lemon squeezed into it. This will give a kick-start to the liver. If you wish, return to bed and relax for a while. Do some simple stretching exercises to stimulate your lymphatic system. Run a bath and, while it is running, give yourself a dry skin brush to stimulate your circulation. For breakfast, prepare the Revitalizer juice from the recipe section, diluting it with some filtered or mineral water if necessary. The fruit and vegetables contained in this juice are known for their liver-cleansing properties.

Late morning Have a massage or shiatsu, reflexology or acupressure session, or try a relaxation technique, such as visualization. Eat some fresh fruit, such as an apple, a pear or some grapes, and drink a herbal tea. Go for a gentle walk before lunchtime.

Lunch Prepare the Energizer juice and have it with a large salad, made from salad leaves, dandelion leaves, rocket, fennel, carrot and beetroot, with a dressing made from olive oil, crushed garlic and lemon juice.

Afternoon Relax for a while after lunch. Try some gentle exercise, such as yoga, Pilates, stretching, walking, cycling or swimming. Make sure that you drink plenty of filtered or mineral water after exercising.

Teatime Make yourself the Red For Go juice. The natural fructose contained in this juice will provide an extra energy boost.

Above: To gain the full health benefits of fresh juices, they should be drunk as soon as they are made because their vitamin levels soon begin to diminish.

Evening Try to eat your evening meal between 6 and 8 pm. Eat some lightly steamed vegetables, including cabbage, carrots and asparagus, sprinkled with chopped fresh herbs and lemon juice, accompanied by organic brown rice. Alternatively, choose a vegetable stir-fry or, if you prefer raw vegetables, opt for a large mixed salad with alfalfa sprouts. After your meal, meditate or practise a relaxation technique. Have an aromatherapy or sitz bath and retire to bed early.

Above: A fresh fruit salad will rejuvenate the system and provide plenty of vitamins.

DAYS FOUR TO EIGHT
Have just one Epsom salts bath during this period. (You should have a maximum of three Epsom salts baths during this two-week detox.)

Morning On waking, follow the same routine that you have followed for the past two days, but for breakfast prepare one of the fruit juices in the recipe section, diluting it with some water. Also, include a fruit salad, prepared with three different types of fruit and topped with a spoonful of live natural yogurt. Alternatively, try some stewed dried fruit, cooked with slices of fresh root ginger, and served with a spoonful of live natural yogurt.

Late morning Have a snack of fresh or dried fruit, such as an apple, a pear, grapes or raisins. Drink a herbal tea. Go for a walk before lunchtime.

Lunch Choose one of the following meals from the recipe section: a large salad, sprinkled with sunflower seeds with an olive oil and lemon juice dressing; a jacket potato with Hummus and salad; Apple and Beetroot Salad with Red Leaves with a jacket potato and Hummus; Stir-fried Beansprouts or Broccoli with Soy Sauce, with brown rice; Hummus with Crudités and a jacket potato; Japanese Salad; one of the soups; or a globe artichoke, dressed with olive oil, lemon juice and crushed garlic with a jacket potato.

Afternoon Rest after eating lunch. If you can, do some gentle exercises later in the afternoon, such as yoga, Pilates, stretching, body-conditioning, swimming, cycling or walking. Drink a herbal tea.

Teatime Choose one of the vegetable juices from the recipe section or, alternatively, snack on some vegetable crudités, a handful of mixed sunflower and pumpkin seeds or a small handful of walnuts, almonds and hazelnuts.

Above: Tomato and Fresh Basil Soup provides valuable antioxidants and will aid the digestive system.

Evening Choose a salad from the recipe section, served with a baked potato, buckwheat noodles or organic brown rice; or one of the light and cleansing meals from the recipe section. Conclude your meal with a cleansing detox dessert.

Above: Strawberries have both cleansing and healing properties and make a nutritious end to a detox meal.

DAYS NINE AND TEN
Follow the detox guidelines given for the weekend detox programme, having only one Epsom salts bath. (This should be your final Epsom salts bath during this two-week detox.)

DAYS ELEVEN TO FOURTEEN
Repeat the routine followed on days four to eight. Try to eat a wide variety of cleansing foods, including beans, grains (not wheat), nuts, seeds and plenty of fresh fruit and vegetables. You can also introduce a small amount of steamed or grilled fish or chicken and the occasional boiled or poached egg on these days, but do not feel tempted to over-indulge. Do not have an Epsom salts bath during this period.

THE DAY AFTER DETOXING
Follow the recommendations given for the one-day mono diet.

Note: A well-balanced diet is vital for good health. The detox diets in this book are restrictive and should only be followed occasionally, and for no longer than recommended.

Many of the detox recipes are intended to serve four people but they can be divided, depending on the number of servings required.

JUICES

Freshly-squeezed juices make up a vital part of any detox programme. They have a powerful effect, stimulating the whole system and encouraging the elimination of toxins. Choose from a classic fruit combination, such as Citrus Shake or Sunrise, or a slightly more unusual mixture of vegetable juices, such as Red for Go or Super Clean. Juices are best made using a juicer. Though they can be made without, the final result tends to have a high fibre content.

Apple Rise

Apples are good for removing impurities from the liver.

INGREDIENTS

Serves 1
1 apple
½ honeydew melon
90g/3½oz red grapes
15ml/1 tbsp lemon juice

1 Quarter the apple. Cut the melon into quarters, remove the seeds and slice the flesh away from the skin. Juice the fruit, then stir in the lemon juice.

— NUTRITION NOTES —

Per portion:

Energy	115kcals/490kJ
Protein	0.8g
Fat, total	0.2g
saturated fat	0g
Carbohydrate	29.5g
Fibre	0g
Sugar	29.5g

— COOK'S TIP —

To blend this juice, remove the apple peel, core and pips.

Melon Pick-me-up

The ingredients in this reviving juice will stimulate the circulation.

INGREDIENTS

Serves 1
2 pears
½ Galia melon
2.5cm/1in piece fresh
 ginger root

1 Quarter the pears, then quarter the melon, remove the seeds and slice the flesh away from the skin. Juice the fruit and ginger.

— NUTRITION NOTES —

Per portion:

Energy	95kcals/410kJ
Protein	0.2g
Fat, total	0.2g
saturated fat	0g
Carbohydrate	24.7g
Fibre	0.1g
Sugar	24.7g

— HEALTH BENEFITS —

Melons are known to be an effective diuretic and help to cleanse the kidneys.

Sunrise

This fruity tropical cleanser will help to boost the digestive system and the kidneys.

INGREDIENTS

Serves 1
1 small mango, peeled
½ pineapple

1 Cut the mango away from the stone. Cut off the pineapple skin, removing the "eyes", then cut into rough chunks and juice.

— NUTRITION NOTES —

Per portion:

Energy	103kcals/442kJ
Protein	0.8g
Fat, total	0g
saturated fat	0g
Carbohydrate	26.3g
Fibre	0.5g
Sugar	26.3g

— HEALTH BENEFITS —

Cleansing mangoes are rich in vitamin C and betacarotene.

Citrus Shake

This refreshing juice is great for boosting the immune system.

INGREDIENTS

Serves 1
1 pink grapefruit
1 blood orange
30ml/2 tbsp lemon juice

1 Peel the grapefruit and orange and cut them into rough segments. Juice the fruit, then stir in the lemon juice.

— NUTRITION NOTES —

Per portion:

Energy	99kcals/420kJ
Protein	1.2g
Fat, total	0g
saturated fat	0g
Carbohydrate	24.9g
Fibre	0.5g
Sugar	24.9g

— HEALTH BENEFITS —

Citrus fruits are a rich source of vitamin C.

Strawberry Sundae

Relax and enjoy this
soothing start to the day.

INGREDIENTS

Serves 1
225g/8oz/2 cups
  strawberries
1 peach or nectarine

— NUTRITION NOTES —	
Per portion:	
Energy	142kcals/607kJ
Protein	0.9g
Fat, total	0.3g
saturated fat	0g
Carbohydrate	36.3g
Fibre	0.1g
Sugar	36.3g

1 Hull the strawberries,
then cut the peach or
nectarine into quarters
around the stone and pull
the fruit apart. Pull out the
stone and cut into rough
slices or chunks. Juice the
strawberries and peach or
nectarine, using a juicer, or
blend for a thicker juice.

Tropical Soother

This reviving juice helps
the liver and kidneys.

INGREDIENTS

Serves 1
1 papaya
½ Cantaloupe melon
90g/3½oz white grapes

— NUTRITION NOTES —	
Per portion:	
Energy	104kcals/444kJ
Protein	1.5g
Fat, total	0g
saturated fat	0g
Carbohydrate	25.5g
Fibre	0.3g
Sugar	25.5g

1 Halve and skin the
papaya, then remove
the seeds using a teaspoon
and cut into rough slices.
Cut open the melon and
remove the seeds with a
spoon. Cut into quarters and
slice the flesh away from the
skin, then cut into rough
chunks. Juice the fruit.

Energizer

Summer Tonic

INGREDIENTS

Serves 1

2 apples
1 large carrot
50g/2oz cooked beetroot
  in natural juice
90g/3½oz white grapes
1cm/½in piece fresh
  root ginger

— NUTRITION NOTES —

Per portion:

Energy	102kcals/450kJ
Protein	0.2g
Fat, total	0.2g
saturated fat	0g
Carbohydrate	26.7g
Fibre	0g
Sugar	26.7g

1 Quarter the apples and top and tail the carrot. Juice the fruit, vegetables and ginger.

— HEALTH BENEFITS —

Beetroot is one of the most effective liver-cleansing vegetables. It is a very good detoxifier and laxative.

INGREDIENTS

Serves 1

3 large vine-ripened tomatoes
½ Little Gem lettuce
5cm/2in piece cucumber
1 small garlic clove
small handful of fresh
  parsley, stalks included
15ml/1 tbsp lemon juice

— NUTRITION NOTES —

Per portion:

Energy	35kcals/155kJ
Protein	2g
Fat, total	0g
saturated fat	0g
Carbohydrate	7.5g
Fibre	1.5g
Sugar	7.5g

1 Halve the tomatoes and lettuce. Peel and chop the cucumber. Juice all the ingredients together.

— HEALTH BENEFITS —

The many nutrients in lettuce include betacarotene, iron and folic acid.

Green Leaves

This rejuvenating juice is exceptionally effective.

INGREDIENTS

Serves 1
1 apple
150g/5oz white grapes
small handful of fresh
    coriander, stalks included
30g/1oz watercress
15ml/1 tbsp lime juice

1 Quarter the apple. Juice the fruit, herbs and watercress, then stir in the lime juice.

— NUTRITION NOTES —

Per portion:

Energy	116kcals/510kJ
Protein	0.8g
Fat, total	0.2g
saturated fat	0g
Carbohydrate	33.3g
Fibre	0.2g
Sugar	33.3g

— HEALTH BENEFITS —

Grapes are one of the most effective detoxifiers and are excellent for treating skin, liver and kidney disorders.

Red For Go

Cleansing apples and fennel make a delicious combination.

INGREDIENTS

Serves 1
½ small red cabbage
½ fennel bulb
2 apples
15ml/1 tbsp lemon juice

1 Roughly slice the cabbage and fennel and quarter the apples. Juice the vegetables and fruit, then stir in the lemon juice.

— NUTRITION NOTES —

Per portion:

Energy	84kcals/360kJ
Protein	0.2g
Fat, total	0.2g
saturated fat	0.2g
Carbohydrate	21.7g
Fibre	0.3g
Sugar	21.7g

— HEALTH BENEFITS —

Fennel is a natural diuretic and raw cabbage has antiviral and antibacterial properties.

Super Clean

This delicious drink will kick-start your system!

INGREDIENTS

Serves 1
3 carrots
30g/1oz young spinach
115g/4oz cooked beetroot
    in natural juice
2 celery sticks

1 Top and tail the carrots. Juice the vegetables.

— NUTRITION NOTES —

Per portion:

Energy	60kcals/257kJ
Protein	1.3g
Fat, total	0.3g
saturated fat	0g
Carbohydrate	14.3g
Fibre	0g
Sugar	14.3g

— HEALTH BENEFITS —

Carrots are another key detox vegetable. Not only do they cleanse, nourish and stimulate the body, but they contain a rich supply of antioxidants.

Revitalizer

This classic combination will benefit those with constipation and arthritis.

INGREDIENTS

Serves 1
3 carrots
1 apple
1 orange

1 Top and tail the carrots, then quarter the apple. Peel the orange and cut into rough segments. Juice the carrots and fruit.

— NUTRITION NOTES —

Per portion:

Energy	121kcals/525kJ
Protein	0.3g
Fat, total	0.3g
saturated fat	0g
Carbohydrate	31.7g
Fibre	0.2g
Sugar	31.7g

— HEALTH BENEFITS —

Natural fruit sugars will provide a boost of energy.

SOUPS

Whether you are following a detox plan or simply enjoy a bowl

of steaming soup, you are sure to find temptation in this chapter.

With a choice of wholesome, chunky soups, such as Roasted Root

Vegetable Soup and North African Spiced Soup, and a selection

of lighter cleansing broths, such as Seaweed Broth with Lemon and

Walnut Noodles and Hot-and-sour Soup, there really is a soup

to suit every mood and taste.

Japanese-style Noodle Soup

This delicate, fragrant soup is perfect for a light lunch. The combination of health-giving miso with nutrient-rich carrots, onions and mushrooms creates the ideal detox soup.

Ingredients

Serves 4

45ml/3 tbsp mugi miso
200g/7oz/scant 2 cups udon noodles, soba noodles or Chinese noodles
30ml/2 tbsp mirin
15ml/1 tbsp lemon juice
30ml/2 tbsp Japanese soy sauce
115g/4oz asparagus tips or mangetouts, thinly sliced diagonally
50g/2oz/scant 1 cup shiitake mushrooms, stalks removed and thinly sliced
1 carrot, sliced into julienne strips
3 spring onions, thinly sliced diagonally
freshly ground black pepper

1 Bring 1 litre/1¾ pints/4 cups water to the boil in a saucepan. Pour 150ml/¼ pint/⅔ cup of the boiling water over the miso and stir until dissolved, then set aside.

2 Meanwhile, bring another large pan of water to the boil, add the noodles and cook according to the packet instructions until just tender.

3 Drain the noodles in a colander and rinse under cold running water.

4 Add the mirin, lemon juice and soy sauce to the saucepan of boiling water. Boil gently for about 3 minutes, then reduce the heat and stir in the dissolved miso mixture.

5 Add the sliced asparagus tips or mangetouts, mushrooms, carrot and spring onions, and simmer for about 2 minutes until just tender. Season with freshly ground black pepper to taste.

6 Divide the cooked noodles among four warmed bowls and carefully ladle the soup over the top of them. Serve immediately.

Health Benefits

Miso is derived from the soya bean and shares many of its health-giving properties. It has been shown to be effective in the fight against stomach cancer, which probably stems from its antioxidant qualities. Studies have also shown that eating miso on a regular basis can increase the body's natural resistance to radiation.

Nutrition Notes

Per portion:

Energy	225kcals/952kJ
Protein	9.4g
Fat, total	4.3g
saturated fat	1.2g
Carbohydrate	57g
Fibre	6.6g
Sugar	2.8g

Seaweed Broth with Lemon and Walnut Noodles

Sea vegetables are rich in minerals and nutrients and have powerful cleansing and healing qualities. Arame lends a sweet, mild flavour to this light but nourishing broth.

INGREDIENTS

Serves 4

75g/3oz/⅓ cup somen noodles
1 large carrot, peeled and shredded
500ml/18fl oz/2¼ cups dashi, or light vegetable stock
15g/½oz arame or hijiki dried seaweed, soaked
50g/2oz enokitaki mushrooms
5ml/1 tsp lemon juice
10ml/2 tsp walnut oil
1 spring onion, green part only, sliced

1 Cook the noodles and carrot in boiling water for 3–4 minutes. Drain and cool under running water.

2 Bring the dashi or stock to the boil, add the arame or seaweed and simmer for 20 minutes.

3 Add the cooked somen noodles and carrot, mushrooms, lemon juice and walnut oil to the saucepan of seaweed and briefly reheat.

4 Divide the soup evenly among four warmed bowls, scatter with spring onion and serve straight away.

COOK'S TIP

The enokitaki mushroom is a cultivated variety and is available from Japanese supermarkets worldwide. Dried seaweed and somen noodles can be found in most health food stores.

NUTRITION NOTES

Per portion:

Energy	95kcals/405kJ
Protein	2.6g
Fat, total	2.7g
saturated fat	0.6g
Carbohydrate	14.3g
Fibre	1.6g
Sugar	1.1g

Hot-and-sour Soup

This light and invigorating Thai soup can help to stimulate the appetite and is easy to digest.

INGREDIENTS

Serves 4

2 carrots
900ml/1½ pints/3¾ cups
    vegetable stock
2.5cm/1in piece fresh root ginger,
    peeled and cut into fine strips
2 lemon grass stalks, outer leaves
    removed and each stalk cut
    into 3 pieces
4 kaffir lime leaves
2 garlic cloves, finely chopped
4 spring onions, finely sliced
5ml/1 tsp sugar
juice of 1 lime
45ml/3 tbsp chopped fresh coriander
130g/3½oz/1 cup Japanese
    tofu, sliced
few shreds red and green pepper and
    carrot slices, to garnish

1 To make carrot flowers, cut each carrot in half crossways, then, using a sharp knife, cut four v-shaped channels lengthways. Slice the carrots into thin rounds and set aside.

COOK'S TIP

Kaffir lime leaves have a distinctive citrus flavour. The fresh leaves can be bought from Asian shops, and some supermarkets now sell them dried.

2 Pour the vegetable stock into a large saucepan. Add the strips of root ginger to the pan with the lemon grass, lime leaves, garlic and half the spring onions. Bring to the boil, then reduce the heat and simmer for about 20 minutes. Strain the stock and discard the flavourings.

3 Return the flavoured stock to the pan, add the reserved spring onions, the sugar, lime juice and chopped fresh coriander.

4 Simmer for 5 minutes, then add the carrot flowers and tofu, and cook for a further 2 minutes until the carrot is just tender. Serve hot.

HEALTH BENEFITS

Tofu is rich in minerals, particularly iron and calcium, and is low in saturated fat. It is an excellent high-protein alternative to meat and dairy products and is highly nutritious and easy to digest, making it the ideal detox food.

NUTRITION NOTES

Per portion:

Energy	139kcals/582kJ
Protein	3g
Fat, total	1.6g
saturated fat	0g
Carbohydrate	2.1g
Fibre	0.9g
Sugar	1.8g

Borsch

Beetroot is the main ingredient of Borsch and is one of nature's most effective detoxifiers, cleansing both the liver and kidneys. It is also a good source of antioxidants and iron.

INGREDIENTS

Serves 4
900g/2lb uncooked beetroot, peeled
2 carrots, peeled
2 celery sticks
45ml/3 tbsp olive oil
2 onions, sliced
2 garlic cloves, crushed
4 tomatoes, peeled, seeded
  and chopped
1 bay leaf
1 large parsley sprig
2 cloves
4 whole peppercorns
1.2 litres/2 pints/5 cups vegetable stock
150ml/¼ pint/⅔ cup beetroot *kvas*
  (see Cook's Tip) or the liquid from
  pickled beetroot
freshly ground black pepper
live natural yogurt, garnished with
  snipped fresh chives or sprigs of
  dill, to serve

1 Cut the beetroot, carrots and celery into fairly thick strips. Heat the oil in a large pan and cook the onions over a low heat for 5 minutes, stirring them occasionally.

2 Add the shreds of beetroot, carrots and celery and cook for a further 5 minutes, stirring occasionally.

3 Add the crushed garlic and chopped tomatoes to the pan and cook, stirring, for 2 minutes more.

4 Tie the bay leaf, parsley, cloves and peppercorns in a piece of muslin.

5 Add the bag of herbs to the pan with the vegetable stock. Bring to the boil, cover and simmer for 1¼ hours, or until the vegetables are very tender. Discard the bag. Stir in the beetroot kvas and pepper. Bring to the boil. Serve in bowls with yogurt garnished with herbs, if liked.

COOK'S TIP

Beetroot *kvas*, fermented juice, adds colour and tartness. If unavailable, peel and grate 1 beetroot, add 150ml/¼ pint/⅔ cup stock and 10ml/2 tsp lemon juice. Bring to the boil, cover and strain after 30 minutes.

NUTRITION NOTES

Per portion:

Energy	145kcals/615kJ
Protein	6.8g
Fat, total	3.5g
saturated fat	0.5g
Carbohydrate	23.1g
Fibre	5.9g
Sugar	20.4g

Fresh Cabbage Soup

This hearty, warming soup is good for the digestion.

INGREDIENTS

Serves 4

1 small turnip
2 carrots
45ml/3 tbsp olive oil
1 large onion, sliced
2 celery sticks, sliced
1 white cabbage, about
    675g/1½lb, shredded
1.2 litres/2 pints/5 cups vegetable stock
1 sharp eating apple, cored, peeled
    and chopped
2 bay leaves
5ml/1 tsp chopped fresh parsley
10ml/2 tsp pickled cucumber juice
    or lemon juice
freshly ground black pepper
fresh herbs, to garnish
live natural yogurt and rye bread,
    to serve

1 Cut the turnip and carrots into matchstick strips. Heat the oil in a large pan and fry the turnip, carrots, onion and celery for 10 minutes.

--- COOK'S TIP ---

Create a rich, red, super-detox version of this cleansing soup by substituting the carrots with beetroot and the white cabbage with red cabbage.

2 Coarsley shred the cabbage, and add to the pan. Pour in the vegetable stock, add the chopped apple, bay leaves and chopped parsley and bring to the boil. Cover and simmer for 40 minutes or until the vegetables are really tender.

3 Remove and discard the bay leaves, then stir in the pickled cucumber juice or lemon juice and season with freshly ground black pepper. Serve hot, garnished with fresh herbs and accompanied by live natural yogurt and rye bread.

--- HEALTH BENEFITS ---

Cabbage is an excellent detoxifier and is reputed to aid the digestion, detoxify the stomach and upper bowels, cleanse the liver and reduce the risk of certain cancers. It is also rich in folate, vitamins C and E, potassium, iron, betacarotene and thiamin, and is well known for its potent antiviral and antibacterial qualities.

--- NUTRITION NOTES ---

Per portion:

Energy	163kcals/651kJ
Protein	5.2g
Fat, total	9.1g
saturated fat	1.2g
Carbohydrate	15.8g
Fibre	5.6g
Sugar	14.1g

Ribollita

This Italian soup is rather like minestrone, but includes beans instead of pasta. It contains a healthy and cleansing combination of onions, garlic, celery, fennel, herbs and beans. Beans are low in fat and high in fibre, and can help control blood sugar levels.

INGREDIENTS

Serves 6
45ml/3 tbsp olive oil
2 onions, chopped
2 carrots, sliced
4 garlic cloves, crushed
2 celery sticks, thinly sliced
1 fennel bulb, trimmed
    and chopped
2 large courgettes, thinly sliced
400g/14oz can chopped tomatoes
30ml/2 tbsp pesto
900ml/1½ pints/3¾ cups
    vegetable stock
400g/14oz can haricot or
    borlotti beans, drained
freshly ground black pepper

To serve
450g/1lb young spinach
15ml/1 tbsp extra virgin olive oil,
    plus extra for drizzling (optional)

1 Heat the oil in a large saucepan. Add the onions, carrots, garlic, celery and fennel and fry gently for 10 minutes. Add the courgettes and fry for a further 2 minutes.

2 Add the tomatoes, pesto, stock and beans and bring to the boil. Reduce the heat, cover and simmer for 25–30 minutes, until the vegetables are tender. Season with pepper to taste.

3 To serve, fry the spinach in the oil for 2 minutes and divide among the soup bowls. Ladle the soup over the spinach and drizzle with oil, if you like.

NUTRITION NOTES

Per portion:

Energy	172kcals/719kJ
Protein	9.3g
Fat, total	6.9g
saturated fat	1g
Carbohydrate	19g
Fibre	7.8g
Sugar	8.5g

VARIATION

Use other dark greens, such as chard or cabbage instead of the spinach; shred and cook in the oil until tender.

HEALTH BENEFITS

The rich dose of garlic in this soup provides the body with an excellent natural cleanser. Garlic also has antiviral, antifungal and antibacterial properties.

Tomato and Fresh Basil Soup

A soup for late summer when fresh tomatoes are at their most flavoursome. Tomatoes provide valuable amounts of antioxidant vitamins, while their classic partner, basil, aids digestion and calms the nervous system.

INGREDIENTS

Serves 4

45ml/3 tbsp olive oil
1 onion, finely chopped
900g/2lb ripe Italian plum tomatoes, roughly chopped
1 garlic clove, roughly chopped
about 1.5 litres/2½ pints/6¼ cups vegetable stock
30ml/2 tbsp sun-dried tomato paste
30ml/2 tbsp shredded fresh basil, plus a few whole leaves, to garnish
freshly ground black pepper

1 Heat the oil in a large saucepan. Add the onion and cook gently for about 5 minutes, stirring frequently, until softened but not brown.

--- VARIATION ---

The soup can also be served cold. Chill for at least 4 hours and serve in chilled bowls.

2 Stir in the chopped tomatoes and garlic, then add the vegetable stock, sun-dried tomato paste and freshly ground black pepper. Bring to the boil, then lower the heat, half cover the pan and simmer gently for 20 minutes, stirring occasionally.

3 Transfer the soup to a blender or food processor, add the shredded fresh basil and process. Press the blended soup through a sieve into a clean saucepan. Gently heat through, stirring. Do not allow the soup to boil. Add more stock if necessary. Pour into warmed bowls and garnish with fresh basil leaves.

--- NUTRITION NOTES ---

Per portion:

Energy	135kcals/564kJ
Protein	4.1g
Fat, total	8.2g
saturated fat	1.2g
Carbohydrate	9.8g
Fibre	2.7g
Sugar	8.8g

Roasted Root Vegetable Soup

This nutritious soup is packed with health-giving vegetables. Butternut squash is particularly high in betacarotene and potassium, which is essential for the efficient functioning of the cells, nerves and muscles. Carrots also contain high levels of betacarotene and are effective detoxifiers.

INGREDIENTS

Serves 6
50ml/2fl oz/¼ cup olive oil
1 small butternut squash, peeled, seeded and cubed
2 carrots, cut into thick rounds
1 large parsnip, cubed
1 small swede, cubed
2 leeks, thickly sliced
1 onion, quartered
3 bay leaves
4 thyme sprigs, plus extra to garnish
3 rosemary sprigs
1.2 litres/2 pints/5 cups
    vegetable stock
freshly ground black pepper
live natural yogurt, to serve

1 Preheat the oven to 200°C/400°F/ Gas 6. Put the olive oil into a large bowl, then add the prepared vegetables and toss until all the vegetables are coated in olive oil.

2 Spread out the vegetables in a single layer on one large or two small baking sheets. Tuck the herbs among the vegetables.

3 Roast the vegetables for 50 minutes until tender, turning occasionally to ensure even browning. Remove from the oven, discard the herbs and transfer the vegetables to a large saucepan.

4 Pour the stock into the pan and bring to the boil. Reduce the heat, season to taste, then simmer for 10 minutes. Transfer the soup to a food processor or blender (or use a hand blender) and process for a few minutes until thick and smooth.

5 Return the processed soup to the saucepan and gently heat through. Season with freshly ground black pepper and serve with a swirl of live natural yogurt. Garnish each serving with a sprig of thyme.

—————— COOK'S TIP ——————

Dried herbs can be used in place of fresh; use 2.5ml/½ tsp of each type and sprinkle over the vegetables in step 2.

——————— NUTRITION NOTES ———————

Per portion:

Energy	100kcals/415kJ
Protein	2.8g
Fat, total	6.3g
saturated fat	0.9g
Carbohydrate	8.5g
Fibre	3.1g
Sugar	5.7g

Spicy Pumpkin Soup

Pumpkin is popular all over the Mediterranean and is an important ingredient in Middle Eastern cookery, where this recipe originates. Ginger and cumin give the soup its spicy flavour and help to aid digestion.

INGREDIENTS

Serves 4
900g/2lb pumpkin, peeled
 and seeds removed
30ml/2 tbsp olive oil
2 leeks, trimmed and sliced
1 garlic clove, crushed
5ml/1 tsp ground ginger
5ml/1 tsp ground cumin
900ml/1½ pints/3¾ cups
 vegetable stock
freshly ground black pepper
fresh coriander leaves, to garnish
60ml/4 tbsp live natural yogurt,
 to serve

1 Cut the peeled pumpkin into chunks. Heat the olive oil in a large pan and add the sliced leeks and garlic. Cook gently over a low heat until the vegetables are softened.

2 Stir in the ginger and cumin and cook, stirring, for a further minute. Add the pumpkin and the vegetable stock and season with freshly ground black pepper.

3 Bring the soup to the boil and simmer for about 30 minutes, until the pumpkin is tender. Process in batches, if necessary, in a blender or food processor.

4 Warm the soup through again, being careful not to bring to boiling point, and serve in warmed individual bowls, with a swirl of live natural yogurt. Garnish with fresh coriander leaves.

--- COOK'S TIP ---

Add an extra cleansing boost to this soup by stirring in 30ml/2 tbsp chopped coriander leaves before serving.

--- HEALTH BENEFITS ---

As with many orange-fleshed vegetables, pumpkin is rich in vitamin A and betacarotene, which are known to protect against cancer. Ginger is regarded as a potent spice that can aid gastro-intestinal disorders and relieve nausea.

--- NUTRITION NOTES ---

Per portion:

Energy	107kcals/448kJ
Protein	5g
Fat, total	6.4g
saturated fat	1.1g
Carbohydrate	7.8g
Fibre	3.1g
Sugar	5.8g

North African Spiced Soup

This warming, mildly spiced soup contains both potatoes and chick-peas, which provide plenty of sustained energy.

INGREDIENTS

Serves 6

1 large onion, chopped
1.2 litres/2 pints/5 cups vegetable stock
5ml/1 tsp ground cinnamon
5ml/1 tsp ground turmeric
15ml/1 tbsp grated fresh root ginger
pinch cayenne pepper
2 carrots, diced
2 celery sticks, diced
400g/14oz can chopped tomatoes
450g/1lb floury potatoes, diced
5 strands saffron
400g/14oz can chick-peas, drained
30ml/2 tbsp chopped fresh coriander
15ml/1 tbsp lemon juice
freshly ground black pepper
wedges of lemon, to serve

1 Place the onion in a large pot with 300ml/½ pint/1¼ cups of the vegetable stock. Simmer gently for about 10 minutes.

— NUTRITION NOTES —	
Per portion:	
Energy	165kcals/699kJ
Protein	8.6g
Fat, total	2.6g
saturated fat	0.3g
Carbohydrate	28.7g
Fibre	5.2g
Sugar	4.9g

2 Meanwhile, mix together the cinnamon, turmeric, ginger and cayenne pepper. Add 30ml/2 tbsp of the vegetable stock and mix together to form a paste.

3 Stir the spicy paste into the onion mixture and add the chopped carrots, celery and the remaining vegetable stock.

4 Bring the mixture back to a boil, stirring, and reduce the heat. Cover the saucepan with a lid and gently simmer for a further 5 minutes.

5 Add the tomatoes and potatoes and simmer gently, covered, for 20 minutes. Add the saffron, chick-peas, coriander and lemon juice. Add pepper to taste and, when piping hot, serve with wedges of lemon.

— HEALTH BENEFITS —
The chick-peas in this soup are a good source of fibre, which can relieve constipation. They are also a good source of low-fat protein, vitamins and minerals.

SALADS

Refreshing salads play an important role in the weekend detox,

the seven-day detox and the two-week liver-cleansing diet.

The wonderful choice of fresh and cooked salads in this chapter will

help to ease you gently through whichever programme you choose.

Try nutrient-packed Late Summer Vegetables in a Hazelnut

Dressing, sustaining Beetroot and Potato Salad or light and cleansing

Apple and Beetroot Salad with Red Leaves.

Spinach and Roast Garlic Salad

Don't worry about the large amount of garlic in this salad. Roasting garlic subdues its flavour. It will lose its pungent taste, becoming sweet and subtle and providing all of the health benefits without the after-effects.

INGREDIENTS

Serves 4
12 garlic cloves,
   unpeeled
60ml/4 tbsp extra virgin
   olive oil
450g/1lb baby spinach leaves
50g/2oz/½ cup pine nuts,
   lightly toasted
juice of ½ lemon
freshly ground black pepper

1 Preheat the oven to 190°C/375°F/Gas 5. Place the unpeeled garlic cloves in a small roasting dish, drizzle over 30ml/2 tbsp of the olive oil and toss to coat evenly.

2 Bake for about 15 minutes until the garlic cloves become slightly charred around the edges.

3 While still warm, tip the garlic cloves, still in their skins, into a salad bowl. Add the spinach, pine nuts, lemon juice and remaining olive oil. Toss well and season with freshly ground black pepper to taste.

4 Serve immediately, squeezing the softened garlic purée out of the skins to eat.

HEALTH BENEFITS

Spinach is a superb source of nutrients, providing a rich supply of antioxidant betacarotene, vitamin C, calcium, folate and iron. Spinach offers the greatest health benefits when eaten raw. Garlic is believed to aid circulation and help fight infections.

COOK'S TIP

If spinach is to be served raw in a salad, the leaves need to be young and tender. Wash them well, drain and pat them dry with kitchen paper.

NUTRITION NOTES

Per portion:

Energy	221kcals/924kJ
Protein	5.6g
Fat, total	20.2g
saturated fat	2.2g
Carbohydrate	3.8g
Fibre	3g
Sugar	2.3g

Date, Orange and Carrot Salad

A colourful and unusual salad with exotic ingredients – fresh dates and orange flower water – combined with crisp leaves, carrots, oranges and toasted almonds. This delicious combination of detoxifying fruit and vegetables will not only stimulate the body's cleansing processes but will provide an energy boost as well.

INGREDIENTS

Serves 4
1 Little Gem lettuce
2 carrots, finely grated
2 oranges
115g/4oz fresh dates, stoned and
   cut into eighths, lengthways
25g/1oz/¼ cup toasted whole
   almonds, chopped
30ml/2 tbsp lemon juice
15ml/1 tbsp orange
   flower water

1 Separate the lettuce leaves, wash and pat dry, then arrange them in a salad bowl or on individual serving plates. Place the grated carrot in a mound on top.

2 Peel the oranges and cut them into segments. Arrange them around the mound of grated carrot. Pile the dates on top, then sprinkle with the toasted almonds. Mix together the lemon juice and orange flower water and sprinkle over the salad. Serve the salad chilled.

VARIATION

You can vary the taste of this delicious salad without affecting its cleansing properties by substituting the oranges with another citrus fruit, such as pink grapefruit, clementines or ugli fruit.

HEALTH BENEFITS

Raw carrots are one of the most effective detoxifiers, working particularly on the liver and kidneys. Oranges aid digestion and are rich in vitamin C.

NUTRITION NOTES

Per portion:

Energy	138kcals/577kJ
Protein	3.1g
Fat, total	3.8g
saturated fat	0.2g
Carbohydrate	24.5g
Fibre	3.3g
Sugar	22.4g

Late Summer Vegetables in a Hazelnut Dressing

This nutrient-packed salad makes a perfect detox lunch or supper.

INGREDIENTS

Serves 4

30ml/2 tbsp olive oil
1 shallot, chopped
1 celery stick, sliced
225g/8oz assorted wild and cultivated
   mushrooms such as young ceps, bay,
   chanterelles, trimmed and sliced
freshly ground black pepper
175g/6oz small potatoes, scrubbed
115g/4oz French beans, trimmed
115g/4oz baby carrots, trimmed
   and peeled
50g/2oz baby sweetcorn, trimmed
50g/2oz asparagus spears
115g/4oz/1 cup broad beans
45ml/3 tbsp hazelnut oil
15ml/1 tbsp groundnut oil
15ml/1 tbsp lemon juice
5ml/1 tsp chopped fresh thyme
50g/2oz hazelnuts, toasted
   and chopped

1 Fry the shallot and celery in olive oil until soft but without colouring. Add the mushrooms and cook over a moderate heat until their juices begin to run, then increase the heat to boil off the juices. Add freshly ground black pepper and set aside.

--- COOK'S TIP ---

To enjoy this salad all year round adapt the vegetables according to what is available and the season.

2 In separate steaming baskets, steam the potatoes for 20 minutes, the beans, carrots, sweetcorn and asparagus for 6 minutes and the broad beans for 3 minutes. Cool under running water and remove the tough outer skins of the broad beans.

3 Combine the steamed vegetables with the mushrooms, then moisten with the hazelnut and groundnut oils. Add the lemon juice and chopped thyme, season with freshly ground black pepper and scatter the toasted hazelnuts over the top.

--- HEALTH BENEFITS ---

Mushrooms are reputed to be effective in counteracting the effect of pollutants in the body. Oriental mushrooms have been at the centre of much attention because of their powerful antiviral properties, which boost the immune system. Although hazelnuts are high in calories, they provide valuable amounts of B complex vitamins, vitamin E, calcium and iron, as well as essential fatty acids.

--- NUTRITION NOTES ---

Per portion:

Energy	312kcals/1295kJ
Protein	6.7g
Fat, total	25.4g
saturated fat	3.4g
Carbohydrate	15.2g
Fibre	5.5g
Sugar	4.8g

Japanese Salad

Hijiki is a mild-tasting seaweed, which is treasured as one of nature's richest mineral sources. The balance of these minerals is said to counteract high blood pressure and aid digestion. The seaweed has a distinguished reputation in Japan for enhancing beauty and adding lustre to hair.

INGREDIENTS

Serves 4

15g/½oz/½ cup hijiki
250g/9oz/1¼ cups radishes, sliced
　into very thin rounds
1 small cucumber, cut into
　thin sticks
75g/3oz/½ cup beansprouts

For the dressing

15ml/1 tbsp sunflower oil
15ml/1 tbsp toasted sesame oil
5ml/1 tsp reduced-salt
　soy sauce
30ml/2 tbsp rice vinegar
15ml/1 tbsp mirin

1 Place the hijiki in a large bowl and cover with cold water for about 15 minutes until it is rehydrated – it should almost triple in volume when fully rehydrated. Drain, rinse under cold running water and drain again.

2 Place the soaked hijiki in a large saucepan of water. Bring to the boil, then reduce the heat and simmer, uncovered, for about 30 minutes or until tender.

3 Meanwhile, make the dressing. Place the sunflower and sesame oils, soy sauce, vinegar and mirin in a bowl or screw-top jar. Stir or shake thoroughly to combine.

4 Arrange the hijiki in a shallow bowl or platter with the radishes, cucumber and beansprouts. Pour over the dressing and toss lightly.

HEALTH BENEFITS

Alginic acid, which is found in hijiki, binds with heavy metals such as lead, cadmium and mercury in the intestines, successfully eliminating them from the body.

COOK'S TIP

Ensure hijiki seaweed is easy to digest by soaking it for 10-15 minutes before use. This will ensure that its valuable nutrients can be fully absorbed by the body.

NUTRITION NOTES

Per portion:

Energy	68kcals/281kJ
Protein	1.6g
Fat, total	5.7g
saturated fat	0.8g
Carbohydrate	2.7g
Fibre	1g
Sugar	2g

Fennel, Orange and Rocket Salad

This light and refreshing salad is a nutritious combination of fruit, vegetables and green leaves. It has excellent detoxifying properties, as well as a rich supply of health-giving nutrients.

INGREDIENTS

Serves 4
2 oranges
1 fennel bulb
115g/4oz rocket leaves
50g/2oz/⅓ cup black olives

For the dressing
30ml/2 tbsp extra virgin
   olive oil
15ml/1 tbsp lemon juice
1 small garlic clove, crushed
freshly ground black pepper

1 With a vegetable peeler, cut strips of rind from the oranges, leaving the white pith behind. Cut the rind into thin julienne strips and cook in boiling water for a few minutes. Drain and set aside.

2 Peel the oranges, removing all the white pith. Slice them into thin rounds and discard any seeds.

3 Cut the fennel bulb in half lengthways and slice across the bulb as thinly as possible, preferably in a food processor fitted with a slicing disc.

VARIATION

For a warm salad, try cutting thicker slices of fennel, brushing with olive oil and grilling lightly on both sides.

4 Combine the oranges and fennel in a serving bowl and toss with the rocket leaves.

5 Mix together the olive oil, lemon juice, garlic and freshly ground black pepper and pour over the salad, toss together well and leave to stand for a few minutes. Sprinkle with the black olives and the strips of orange rind.

HEALTH BENEFITS

Fennel is a known diuretic and has a calming effect on the stomach. Oranges provide an excellent source of vitamin C.

NUTRITION NOTES

Per portion:

Energy	91kcals/379kJ
Protein	1.3g
Fat, total	7.1g
saturated fat	1g
Carbohydrate	5.9g
Fibre	2.5g
Sugar	5.8g

Warm Vegetable Salad

This salad features raw red pepper and sprouted beans, which make a crunchy contrast to the warm steamed broccoli, green beans and carrots. The delicious combination of raw and lightly cooked vegetables offers a powerhouse of cleansing properties along with long-term energy from the new potatoes.

INGREDIENTS

Serves 2
8 new potatoes
225g/8oz broccoli, cut into
　small florets
200g/7oz/1½ cups fine
　green beans
2 carrots, cut into thin ribbons
　with a vegetable peeler
1 red pepper, seeded and cut
　into strips
50g/2oz/½ cup sprouted beans
sprigs of watercress, to garnish
freshly ground black pepper

For the dressing
45ml/3 tbsp extra virgin
　olive oil
15ml/1 tbsp toasted sesame oil
juice of ½ lemon

1 Bring a saucepan of water to the boil, add the new potatoes and cook for 10–15 minutes, until tender. Drain, leave to cool slightly, then halve or thickly slice the potatoes, depending on their size.

2 Meanwhile, place the broccoli and green beans in a steamer over a saucepan of boiling water and steam for 4–5 minutes until just tender, but still crisp to the bite. When the broccoli and beans are nearly cooked, place the prepared carrots in the steamer with the other vegetables and cook lightly for a further 2 minutes.

3 In a small bowl, mix together the olive oil, sesame oil and lemon juice and season with freshly ground black pepper.

4 Arrange the cooked vegetables on a serving platter with the red pepper and sprouted beans. Garnish with watercress and pour over the dressing.

HEALTH BENEFITS

Sprouted beans are easily digestible and packed with concentrated goodness. Their nutrients include vitamins B, C and E, protein, potassium and phosphorus. When fresh, their vitamin and enzyme content is at its peak, and they are believed to stimulate the body's ability to cleanse itself.

NUTRITION NOTES

Per portion:	
Energy	174kcals/730kJ
Protein	10.3g
Fat, total	2.5g
saturated fat	0.6g
Carbohydrate	29g
Fibre	9.1g
Sugar	13.9g

Moroccan Cooked Salad

This cooked salad features a nutritious combination of tomatoes, onions, cucumber and green pepper. The fresh coriander tastes wonderful and is said to tone the stomach.

INGREDIENTS

Serves 4

2 well-flavoured tomatoes, quartered
2 onions, chopped
½ cucumber, halved lengthways,
    seeded and sliced
1 green pepper, halved, seeded
    and chopped
30ml/2 tbsp lemon juice
45ml/3 tbsp olive oil
2 garlic cloves, crushed
30ml/2 tbsp chopped
    fresh coriander
freshly ground black pepper
sprigs of coriander, to garnish

1 Put the tomatoes, onions, cucumber and green pepper into a pan, add 60ml/4 tbsp water and simmer for 5 minutes. Leave to cool.

COOK'S TIP

Although this salad is delicious cooked, it is just as tasty when the ingredients are left raw and simply tossed in the dressing.

2 Place the lemon juice, olive oil and crushed garlic cloves in a small bowl or jar and stir or shake to combine thoroughly.

3 Strain the cooked vegetables and transfer to a serving bowl. Pour over the dressing, season with freshly ground black pepper to taste and mix lightly to combine. Stir in the chopped coriander. Serve at once, garnished with sprigs of fresh coriander.

HEALTH BENEFITS

Tomatoes are rich in both vitamin C and betacarotene, which have a stimulating effect on the liver. Onions are great for cleansing the system. They have anti-bacterial and antiviral qualities, as well as the ability to relieve bronchial congestion and asthma. Cucumber is one of the best natural diuretics and works to improve the efficiency of the kidneys, to eliminate waste and prevent water retention.

NUTRITION NOTES

Per portion:

Energy	73kcals/302kJ
Protein	1g
Fat, total	5.8g
saturated fat	0.8g
Carbohydrate	4.5g
Fibre	1.4g
Sugar	3.8g

Grated Beetroot and Celery Salad

Both beetroot and celery are effective and well-documented detoxifiers. Celery, in particular, is favoured by advocates of detoxing as it contains very few calories and is recognized as being a diuretic and laxative.

INGREDIENTS

Serves 4
450g/1lb uncooked beetroot,
    peeled and grated
4 celery sticks, finely chopped
30ml/2 tbsp freshly squeezed
    apple juice
fresh herbs, to garnish

For the dressing
45ml/3 tbsp sunflower oil
15ml/1 tbsp cider vinegar
4 spring onions, finely sliced
30ml/2 tbsp chopped
    fresh parsley
freshly ground black pepper

1 Toss the beetroot, celery and apple juice together in a bowl to mix.

2 Put all the ingredients for the dressing in a small bowl and whisk with a fork until well blended. Stir half into the beetroot mixture.

3 Drizzle the remaining dressing over the top. Allow to marinate for at least 2 hours before serving, for the fullest flavour. Garnish with fresh herbs.

VARIATION

Make a lemony dressing: substitute freshly squeezed lemon juice for the cider vinegar in the dressing. Lemon juice is a powerful astringent and cleanser and will help to stimulate the liver.

NUTRITION NOTES

Per portion:

Energy	122kcals/510kJ
Protein	2.3g
Fat, total	8.5g
saturated fat	1g
Carbohydrate	9.9g
Fibre	2.6g
Sugar	9.2g

Beetroot and Potato Salad

This is a brightly coloured salad with a lovely texture. The sweetness of the beetroot contrasts perfectly with the tangy dressing. This salad makes a perfect choice for the seven-day or two-week liver-cleansing diet.

INGREDIENTS

Serves 4
4 beetroot
4 potatoes, peeled and diced
1 red onion, minced
150ml/¼ pint/⅔ cup live
    natural yogurt
10ml/2 tbsp cider vinegar
2 small gherkins, finely chopped
freshly ground black pepper
parsley sprigs, to garnish

1 Place the fresh beetroot in a large saucepan of boiling water. Bring back to boiling point, reduce the heat and cook for about 40 minutes or until just tender. Remove the cooked beetroot from the pan using a slotted spoon and place in a large bowl. Set aside to cool slightly.

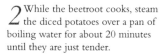

2 While the beetroot cooks, steam the diced potatoes over a pan of boiling water for about 20 minutes until they are just tender.

3 When the beetroot is cool enough to handle, rinse and pull the skins off. Chop into rough pieces and place in a serving bowl. Add the cooked potatoes and the minced onions.

4 In a small bowl, mix together the yogurt, cider vinegar and gherkins. Reserve a few tablespoons of the dressing for a garnish and pour the remainder over the salad. Toss the vegetables and yogurt mixture together and serve garnished with parsley sprigs and the remaining dressing.

HEALTH BENEFITS

Potatoes provide a steady rise in blood sugar, ensuring sustained energy, which is essential when following a detox plan. Beetroot is an effective detoxifier and is particularly good for cleansing the liver. Its high fibre content can relieve constipation.

NUTRITION NOTES

Per portion:

Energy	74kcals/312kJ
Protein	3.5g
Fat, total	0.5g
saturated fat	0.2g
Carbohydrate	14.6g
Fibre	1.4g
Sugar	6.6g

White Bean Salad with Red Pepper Dressing

The speckled herb and red pepper dressing adds a wonderful colour contrast to this salad, which is best served warm. Perfect for a detox or healthy summer lunch, this salad will provide a steady stream of energy.

INGREDIENTS

Serves 4

1 large red pepper
60ml/4 tbsp olive oil
1 large garlic clove, crushed
25g/1oz/1 cup fresh oregano
   leaves or flat leaf parsley
15ml/1 tbsp lemon juice
400g/14oz/3 cups canned
   flageolet beans, drained
   and rinsed
200g/7oz/1½ cups canned
   cannellini beans, drained
   and rinsed
freshly ground black pepper

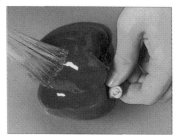

1 Preheat the oven to 200°C/400°F/ Gas 6. Place the red pepper on a baking sheet, brush with oil and roast for 30 minutes or until wrinkled and soft.

--- HEALTH BENEFITS ---

Pulses, such as cannellini beans, are low in fat and high in fibre and protein and should be a regular part of a healthy balanced diet. They are also a good source of many minerals, including iron, potassium, phosphorus and magnesium, as well as B complex vitamins.

2 Remove the pepper from the oven and place in a plastic bag. Seal the bag and leave to cool. (This makes the skin easier to remove.)

3 When the pepper is cool enough to handle, remove it from the bag and carefully peel off the skin. Rinse the peeled pepper under running water.

4 Slice the pepper in half and remove the seeds and stem, gently using a knife to scrape away the membrane that holds the seeds in place. Dice the pepper, retaining any juices. Set aside.

5 Heat the remaining olive oil in a saucepan and cook the garlic for about 1 minute until softened. Remove from the heat, then add the oregano or parsley, the roasted red pepper and any retained juices, and the lemon juice. Stir together gently.

6 Put the flageolet and cannellini beans in a large serving bowl and pour over the dressing. Season to taste with freshly ground black pepper, then stir gently until combined. Serve warm.

--- NUTRITION NOTES ---

Per portion:

Energy	249kcals/1044kJ
Protein	10.2g
Fat, total	12g
saturated fat	1.7g
Carbohydrate	26.7g
Fibre	9.1g
Sugar	6.4g

Bulgur Wheat Salad with Walnuts and Herbs

INGREDIENTS

Serves 4

225g/8oz/1 generous cup
  bulgur wheat
350ml/12fl oz/1½ cups vegetable stock
1 cinnamon stick
generous pinch of ground cumin
pinch of cayenne pepper
pinch of ground cloves
10 mangetouts, topped and tailed
1 red and 1 yellow pepper, roasted,
  skinned, seeded and diced
2 plum tomatoes, peeled, seeded
  and diced
2 shallots, finely sliced
5 black olives, stoned and cut
  into quarters
30ml/2 tbsp each shredded fresh basil,
  mint and parsley
30ml/2 tbsp roughly chopped walnuts
30ml/2 tbsp lemon juice
30ml/1fl oz/2 tbsp olive oil
freshly ground black pepper
onion rings, to garnish

1 Place the bulgur wheat in a large bowl. Pour the vegetable stock into a saucepan, add the cinnamon, cumin, cayenne pepper and ground cloves and bring to the boil.

HEALTH BENEFITS

This well-balanced, nutritious dish combines a good mixture of grains, fresh vegetables, nuts and herbs. It is perfect for a cleansing lunch or a light evening meal.

---

2 Cook the spices and stock for 1 minute, then pour the stock over the bulgur wheat and leave to stand for 30 minutes.

3 In another bowl, mix together the mangetouts, roasted peppers, tomatoes, shallots, olives, herbs and walnuts. Add the lemon juice, olive oil and a little freshly ground black pepper. Stir thoroughly to mix.

4 Strain the bulgur wheat, shaking to remove as much liquid as possible, and discard the cinnamon stick. Place in a large serving bowl, stir in the fresh vegetable mixture and serve, garnished with onion rings.

NUTRITION NOTES

Per portion:

Energy	326kcals/1363kJ
Protein	7.8g
Fat, total	10.7g
saturated fat	1.2g
Carbohydrate	54.1g
Fibre	3.8g
Sugar	8.1g

Spiced Potato Salad with Mango Dressing

This sweet and spicy salad makes a wonderful accompaniment to a mixed leaf salad.

INGREDIENTS

Serves 4
15ml/1 tbsp olive oil
1 onion, sliced into rings
1 garlic clove, crushed
5ml/1 tsp ground cumin
5ml/1 tsp ground coriander
1 mango, peeled, stoned
   and diced
25g/1oz/2 tbsp organic honey
30ml/2 tbsp lime juice
900g/2lb new potatoes, cut in
   half and boiled
15ml/1 tbsp sesame seeds
freshly ground black pepper
fresh coriander, to garnish

1 Heat the olive oil in a frying pan and gently fry the onion and garlic over a low heat for about 10 minutes.

2 Stir in the cumin and coriander, and fry for a few seconds. Stir in the mango and fry for 5 minutes. Remove from the heat. Stir in the honey and lime juice and season.

NUTRITION NOTES	
Per portion:	
Energy	247kcals/1041kJ
Protein	5.9g
Fat, total	5.5g
saturated fat	0.7g
Carbohydrate	46.3g
Fibre	4.4g
Sugar	8.4g

3 Place the boiled potatoes in a large serving bowl and spoon the hot mango dressing over them. Toss lightly and sprinkle with sesame seeds. Serve the salad while the dressing is still warm, garnished with the fresh coriander leaves.

LIGHT AND
CLEANSING MEALS

These delicious recipes have been especially selected for their cleansing

qualities. Each recipe uses ingredients that are known to boost the

system and encourage the elimination of toxins. The recipes range

from substantial snacks such as Hummus, and Stuffed Vine Leaves,

to lighter dishes and wholesome meals, including Spring Vegetable

Stir-fry, and Brown Rice Risotto with Mushrooms.

Hummus

This creamy purée combines chick-peas, garlic, lemon juice and sesame seed paste (tahini) to produce a tasty snack or meal.

INGREDIENTS

Serves 4
150g/5oz/¾ cup dried
   chick-peas
juice of 2 lemons
2 garlic cloves, sliced
30ml/2 tbsp olive oil
pinch of cayenne pepper
150ml/¼ pint/⅔ cup tahini
freshly ground black pepper
extra olive oil and cayenne pepper,
   for sprinkling
flat leaf parsley, to garnish
brown rice cakes, to serve

1 Put the chick-peas in a bowl, cover with plenty of cold water and leave to soak overnight.

2 Drain, place in a saucepan and cover with fresh water. Bring to the boil and boil rapidly for 10 minutes. Reduce the heat and simmer gently for about 1 hour until soft. Drain.

3 Process the chick-peas in a food processor or blender until smooth. Add the lemon juice, garlic, olive oil, cayenne pepper and tahini and blend until creamy.

4 Season with pepper and transfer to a serving dish. Sprinkle with oil and cayenne pepper. Garnish with parsley and serve with rice cakes.

NUTRITION NOTES	
Per portion:	
Energy	397kcals/1652kJ
Protein	14.9g
Fat, total	29.6g
saturated fat	4.1g
Carbohydrate	18.9g
Fibre	7g
Sugar	1.1g

Pea Guacamole with Crudités

INGREDIENTS

Serves 4
350g/12oz/3 cups frozen peas,
   completely defrosted
1 garlic clove, crushed
2 spring onions, trimmed and chopped
5ml/1 tsp finely grated rind and juice
   of 1 lime
2.5ml/½ tsp ground cumin
dash of Tabasco sauce
15ml/1 tbsp extra virgin olive oil
30ml/2 tbsp chopped fresh coriander
freshly ground black pepper
pinch of cayenne and lime slices,
   to garnish

For the crudités
6 baby carrots
2 celery sticks
1 red-skinned eating apple
1 pear
15ml/1 tbsp lemon or lime juice
6 baby sweetcorn

1 Put the peas, garlic, spring onions, lime rind and juice, cumin, Tabasco sauce, olive oil and freshly ground black pepper into a food processor or a blender and process for a few minutes until smooth.

2 Add the chopped fresh coriander and process for a few more seconds. Spoon into a serving bowl, cover with clear film and place in the fridge to chill for about 30 minutes, to allow the flavours to develop.

3 To make the crudités, trim and peel the carrots and quarter lengthways. Halve the celery sticks lengthways and trim to the same length as the carrots. Quarter, core and thickly slice the apple and pear, then dip into the lemon or lime juice. Arrange with the baby sweetcorn in a bowl or on a platter.

4 Sprinkle the cayenne over the guacamole and garnish with the lime slices.

NUTRITION NOTES	
Per portion:	
Energy	86kcals/361kJ
Protein	5.3g
Fat, total	3.6g
saturated fat	0.6g
Carbohydrate	8.6g
Fibre	4.5g
Sugar	2.5g

Stuffed Vine Leaves

This vegetarian version of the famous Greek dish uses a healthy combination of rice, pine nuts and raisins.

Ingredients

Makes about 40
40 fresh vine leaves
60ml/4 tbsp olive oil
lemon wedges and a crisp
  salad, to serve

For the stuffing
150g/5oz/¾ cup long grain
  rice, rinsed
2 bunches spring onions,
  finely chopped
40g/1½oz/¼ cup pine nuts
25g/1oz/scant ¼ cup seedless raisins
30ml/2 tbsp chopped fresh
  mint leaves
60ml/4 tbsp chopped fresh parsley
3.5ml/¾ tsp freshly ground
  black pepper

1 Using a knife, cut out the thick, coarse stems from the vine leaves. Blanch the leaves in a large pan of boiling water until they just begin to change colour, then drain. Refresh in cold water and drain again.

2 Mix all the stuffing ingredients together in a bowl.

3 Open out the vine leaves, ribbed side uppermost. Place a heaped teaspoonful of the stuffing on each.

4 Fold over the two outer edges to prevent the stuffing from falling out, then roll up the vine leaf from the stem end to form a neat roll.

5 Arrange the rolls in the base of a steamer and sprinkle over the oil. Steam for 50–60 minutes, or until the rice is cooked. Serve cold or hot, with salad and lemon wedges.

--- Cook's Tip ---

To boost vitamin, mineral and fibre levels substitute brown rice for white, cooking for an extra 15–20 minutes.

--- Nutrition Notes ---

Per stuffed vine leaf:

Energy	34kcals/142kJ
Protein	0.5g
Fat, total	1.9g
saturated fat	0.2g
Carbohydrate	3.8g
Fibre	0.1g
Sugar	0.6g

Stir-fried Beansprouts

This fresh, crunchy vegetable is an excellent low-fat source of iron. In Chinese medicine, sprouted beans are revered for their ability to cleanse and rejuvenate the system, and they make this a perfect dish for a detoxifying light lunch.

INGREDIENTS

Serves 4

15ml/1 tbsp olive oil
1 garlic clove, finely chopped
5ml/1 tsp grated fresh root ginger
1 small carrot, cut into fine matchsticks
50g/2oz/½ cup drained, canned
   bamboo shoots, cut into
   fine matchsticks
450g/1lb/8 cups beansprouts
15ml/1 tbsp reduced-salt soy sauce
2.5ml/½ tsp sesame oil
freshly ground black pepper

1 Heat the olive oil in a non-stick frying pan or wok. Add the chopped garlic and grated ginger and stir-fry for a few minutes.

NUTRITION NOTES

Per portion:

Energy	72kcals/299kJ
Protein	4g
Fat, total	3.7g
saturated fat	0.5g
Carbohydrate	6.1g
Fibre	2.1g
Sugar	3.5g

2 Add the carrot and bamboo shoot matchsticks to the pan or wok and stir-fry for a few minutes.

3 Add the beansprouts to the pan or wok and season with freshly ground black pepper. Toss the beansprouts over the heat with the other vegetables for about 3 minutes until hot.

4 Sprinkle over the soy sauce and sesame oil, toss to mix thoroughly, then serve at once.

COOK'S TIP

Beansprouts keep best when stored in the fridge in a bowl of cold water, but do change the water daily.

Broccoli with Soy Sauce

Broccoli should form a regular part of your diet. It is extremely nutritious, as it is rich in betacarotene, vitamins, particularly A, C and E, and minerals. It is also said to reduce the risk of certain cancers.

INGREDIENTS

Serves 4
450g/1lb broccoli
15ml/1 tbsp sunflower oil
2 garlic cloves, crushed
15ml/1 tbsp reduced-salt
    soy sauce
fried garlic slices, to
    garnish (optional)

1 Trim off the thick stems from the broccoli, and cut the head part into large florets.

2 Bring a saucepan of water to the boil. Add the broccoli and cook for 3–4 minutes until just tender.

3 Drain the broccoli thoroughly and arrange in a heated serving dish. Heat the oil in a small saucepan. Fry the garlic for 2 minutes, then remove with a slotted spoon. Pour the oil carefully over the broccoli. Drizzle with soy sauce, scatter with fried garlic slices, if you like, and serve.

NUTRITION NOTES	
Per portion:	
Energy	67kcals/277kJ
Protein	5.8g
Fat, total	3.8g
saturated fat	0.6g
Carbohydrate	2.6g
Fibre	2.9g
Sugar	1.7g

Mixed Vegetable Casserole

This hearty casserole features an impressive range of fresh, vitamin-packed vegetables. It will make a delicious and sustaining meal towards the end of a two-week liver-cleansing diet.

INGREDIENTS

Serves 4

1 aubergine
115g/4oz/½ cup okra, cut in
   half lengthways
225g/8oz/2 cups frozen or fresh peas
225g/8oz/1½ cups green beans, cut
   into 2.5cm/1in pieces
4 courgettes, cut into
   1cm/½in pieces
2 onions, finely chopped
450g/1lb old potatoes, diced into
   2.5cm/1in pieces
1 red pepper, seeded and sliced
400g/14oz can chopped tomatoes
150ml/¼ pint/⅔ cup
   vegetable stock
60ml/4 tbsp olive oil
75ml/5 tbsp chopped fresh parsley
5ml/1 tsp paprika

For the topping
3 tomatoes, sliced
1 courgette, sliced

1 Preheat the oven to 190°C/375°F/ Gas 5. Dice the aubergine into 2.5cm/1in pieces. Add the vegetables to a large ovenproof casserole.

2 Add the canned tomatoes, vegetable stock, olive oil, chopped parsley and paprika and combine well.

3 Level the surface of the vegetables with the back of a wooden spoon and arrange alternate slices of tomatoes and courgette on the top in an attractive pattern.

4 Put the lid on or cover the casserole tightly with kitchen foil. Cook in the oven for 50–70 minutes. Serve hot, or leave to cool and serve warm or at room temperature.

HEALTH BENEFITS

The wide variety of fresh vegetables in this dish offers a rich supply of health-giving nutrients. Onions are powerful cleansers and known for their healing properties, while potatoes provide a source of sustained energy. The courgette and tomato topping further boosts the vitamin and fibre content of this dish.

NUTRITION NOTES

Per portion:

Energy	300kcals/1254kJ
Protein	11.1g
Fat, total	13.4g
saturated fat	2.1g
Carbohydrate	36.2g
Fibre	8.7g
Sugar	12.5g

Stir-fried Rice and Vegetables

The ginger gives this Oriental dish a wonderful flavour and also boosts its therapeutic properties.

INGREDIENTS

Serves 2 as a main meal

115g/4oz/generous ½ cup brown basmati rice, rinsed and drained
350ml/12fl oz/1½ cups vegetable stock
2.5cm/1in piece of fresh root ginger, finely sliced
1 garlic clove, halved
5cm/2in piece of pared lemon rind
115g/4oz/1½ cups shiitake mushrooms
30ml/2 tbsp olive oil
175g/6oz baby carrots, trimmed
225g/8oz baby courgettes, halved
175–225g/6–8oz/about 1½ cups broccoli, broken into florets
6 spring onions, diagonally sliced
15ml/1 tbsp reduced-salt soy sauce
10ml/2 tsp toasted sesame oil

1 Put the brown rice in a saucepan and pour in the vegetable stock. Add the root ginger, garlic and lemon rind. Slowly bring to the boil, then cover the pan with a lid and cook very gently for 20–25 minutes until the rice is tender.

2 Drain and remove the garlic, ginger and lemon rind from the rice. Return the rice to the pan and cover with a lid to keep warm. Set aside.

3 Slice the mushrooms, discarding the stems. Heat the olive oil in a wok and stir-fry the carrots for 4–5 minutes until they just start to become tender.

4 Add the mushrooms and baby courgettes and stir-fry for about 3 minutes. Add the broccoli and spring onions and stir-fry for a further 3 minutes, by which time all the vegetables should be tender but still retain a bit of "bite".

5 Add the cooked rice to the wok, and toss briefly with the vegetables over the heat to combine and heat through thoroughly.

6 Sprinkle over the soy sauce and the toasted sesame oil and toss again lightly. Spoon into individual bowls and serve immediately.

HEALTH BENEFITS

Ginger has long been recognized as an excellent detoxifier. It can provide relief for gastro-intestinal disorders, aid indigestion and help to boost the immune system.

The starch in brown rice is absorbed slowly by the body, helping to keep blood sugar levels on an even keel, which is very important during a detox. Brown rice is also good for treating digestive disorders, soothing and cleansing the intestinal tract, calming the nervous system and preventing kidney stones.

NUTRITION NOTES

Per portion:

Energy	445kcals/1869kJ
Protein	15.9g
Fat, total	18.1g
saturated fat	3.4g
Carbohydrate	58.4g
Fibre	7.9g
Sugar	10g

Couscous with Vegetables

Couscous is a light, fluffy grain that readily accepts stronger flavoured ingredients, such as herbs and spices. It makes a great lunch or supper dish.

INGREDIENTS

Serves 4

275g/10oz/1⅔ cups couscous
525ml/18fl oz/2¼ cups boiling
    vegetable stock
16–20 black olives
2 small courgettes
25g/1oz/¼ cup flaked
    almonds, toasted
60ml/4 tbsp olive oil
15ml/1 tbsp lemon juice
15ml/1 tbsp chopped fresh coriander
15ml/1 tbsp chopped fresh parsley
good pinch of ground cumin
good pinch of paprika

1 Place the couscous in a bowl and pour over the boiling vegetable stock. Stir with a fork, then set aside for 10 minutes for the stock to be absorbed. When the stock has been absorbed, fluff the grains with a fork.

NUTRITION NOTES	
Per portion:	
Energy	412kcals/1731kJ
Protein	8.5g
Fat, total	18.1g
saturated fat	2.6g
Carbohydrate	57.4g
Fibre	2.4g
Sugar	1.6g

2 Halve the olives and discard the stones. Top and tail the courgettes and cut into small julienne strips.

3 Add the courgette strips, olives and toasted almonds to the bowl of couscous and gently mix together.

4 Blend together the olive oil, lemon juice, herbs and spices.

5 Pour the dressing over the couscous. Gently stir to combine, and serve.

VARIATION
Add extra flavour to this salad by stirring in 10ml/2 tsp grated fresh root ginger.

Spring Vegetable Stir-fry

Fast, fresh and packed with healthy vegetables, this stir-fry makes an ideal supper dish for either a long or a short detox.

INGREDIENTS

Serves 4

15ml/1 tbsp groundnut or vegetable oil
5ml/1 tsp toasted sesame oil
1 garlic clove, chopped
2.5cm/1in piece fresh root ginger, finely chopped
225g/8oz baby carrots
350g/12oz/3 cups broccoli florets
175g/6oz/⅓ cup asparagus tips
2 spring onions, cut on the diagonal
175g/6oz/1½ cups spring greens, finely shredded
30ml/2 tbsp reduced-salt soy sauce
15ml/1 tbsp freshly squeezed apple juice
15ml/1 tbsp sesame seeds, toasted
noodles, to serve (optional)

1 Heat a frying pan or wok over a high heat. Add the groundnut or vegetable oil and the sesame oil, and reduce the heat. Add the garlic and sauté for 2 minutes.

2 Add the chopped ginger, baby carrots, broccoli and asparagus tips to the pan and stir-fry for about 4 minutes. Add the spring onions and spring greens to the pan and stir-fry for a further 2 minutes.

3 Add the soy sauce and apple juice and cook for 1–2 minutes until the vegetables are tender, adding a little water if they appear dry.

4 Spoon the vegetables into four warmed bowls and sprinkle with toasted sesame seeds. Serve with noodles, if liked.

VARIATION

Vary the taste and texture of this dish by substituting red peppers for the asparagus or spinach for the spring greens.

HEALTH BENEFITS

Green and orange vegetables are an excellent source of vitamins C and E, and betacarotene, which is believed to help in the fight against cancer. Fresh root ginger is one of the top detox spices, helping to stimulate the whole system, and aiding gastro-intestinal disorders.

NUTRITION NOTES

Per portion:

Energy	128kcals/531kJ
Protein	7.7g
Fat, total	7.2g
saturated fat	1.3g
Carbohydrate	8.4g
Fibre	5.8g
Sugar	7.2g

Spiced Turnips with Spinach and Tomatoes

Sweet baby turnips, tender spinach and ripe tomatoes make a tempting combination in this simple Eastern Mediterranean vegetable stew. Whether you want a tasty detox meal or a cleansing supper, this is the perfect dish.

INGREDIENTS

Serves 6

450g/1lb plum or other well-flavoured
    tomatoes
60ml/4 tbsp olive oil
2 onions, sliced
450g/1lb baby turnips, peeled
5ml/1 tsp paprika
60ml/4 tbsp chopped fresh coriander
450g/1lb fresh young spinach,
    stalks removed
freshly ground black pepper

1 Plunge the tomatoes into a bowl of boiling water for 30 seconds, then refresh in a bowl of cold water. Peel away the loosened tomato skins and chop roughly.

2 Heat the olive oil in a large frying pan or sauté pan and fry the onion slices for about 5 minutes until they are golden brown.

3 Add the baby turnips, tomatoes and paprika to the pan with 60ml/ 4 tbsp water, and cook until the tomatoes are pulpy. Cover with a lid and continue cooking until the baby turnips have softened.

4 Stir in the chopped coriander, then add the prepared spinach and a little freshly ground black pepper and continue to cook for 2–3 minutes more until the spinach has wilted. Season with freshly ground black pepper to taste. Serve warm or cold.

HEALTH BENEFITS

Tomatoes help to stimulate the liver and the elimination of toxins and waste, while the spinach provides a valuable supply of vitamin C, folate and iron.

NUTRITION NOTES

Per portion:

Energy	122kcals/507kJ
Protein	3.5g
Fat, total	8.4g
saturated fat	1.2g
Carbohydrate	8.6g
Fibre	4.4g
Sugar	7.9g

Stuffed Celeriac

Celeriac is a root vegetable that is related to celery. It has a similar flavour and shares many of the same health-giving properties. Here, it is partnered with garlic and parsley, both of which are excellent cleansers.

INGREDIENTS

Serves 4

4 small celeriac, about
    200g/7oz each
juice of 2 lemons
150ml/¼ pint/⅔ cup olive oil
lemon wedges and sprigs of flat leaf
    parsley, to garnish

For the stuffing

6 garlic cloves, finely chopped
5ml/1 tsp black peppercorns,
    finely crushed
60–75ml/4–5 tbsp chopped
    fresh parsley

1 Peel the celeriac carefully with a sharp knife and quickly immerse in a bowl of water and lemon juice until ready to use. The lemon juice prevents the celeriac from discolouring.

HEALTH BENEFITS

Like celery, celeriac is reputed to be an effective diuretic, working on the urinary system.

2 Reserving the lemon water, lift out a celeriac and, very carefully, scoop out the flesh, leaving a shell about 2cm/¾in thick, in which to put the filling. Scoop out the remaining celeriac in the same way.

3 Working quickly, chop up the celeriac flesh that has been scooped out and mix with the garlic and peppercorns. Mix in the parsley.

4 Fill the shells with the stuffing and sit the celeriac in a large pan, making sure that they are stable and upright and will not fall over as they cook. Pour in the olive oil and enough lemon water to come about halfway up the celeriac.

5 Cover the pan and simmer very gently for 20–30 minutes, or until the celeriac are tender and nearly all the cooking liquid has been absorbed. Serve the celeriac hot or cold with their juices, and garnish with lemon wedges and sprigs of parsley.

NUTRITION NOTES

Per portion:

Energy	196kcals/836kJ
Protein	2.49g
Fat, total	3.1g
saturated fat	0.6g
Carbohydrate	42.6g
Fibre	4.8g
Sugar	11.4g

Baked Cabbage

This economical dish uses the whole cabbage, including the core where much of its flavour resides. Cabbage has been shown to be a valuable detoxifier, improving the efficiency of the liver and digestive system. It is most effective when eaten raw or juiced, but is still a good cleanser when lightly baked.

INGREDIENTS

Serves 6

1 green or white cabbage,
   about 675g/1½lb
15ml/1 tbsp light olive oil
30ml/2 tbsp water
45–60ml/3–4 tbsp vegetable stock
4 firm, ripe tomatoes, peeled
   and chopped
5ml/1 tsp paprika
15ml/1 tbsp chopped fresh
   parsley or fennel, to
   garnish (optional)

For the topping

3 firm ripe tomatoes,
   thinly sliced
15ml/1 tbsp olive oil
freshly ground black pepper

1 Preheat the oven to 180°C/350°F/ Gas 4. Finely shred the leaves and the core of the cabbage. Heat the olive oil in a frying pan with the water and add the chopped cabbage. Cook over a very low heat, to allow the cabbage to sweat, for 5–10 minutes with the lid on. Stir occasionally.

2 Add the stock to the pan and stir in the chopped tomatoes and paprika. Cook for a further 10 minutes.

3 Tip the cabbage mixture into an ovenproof dish. Level the surface and arrange the sliced tomatoes on top. Add pepper and brush with the oil.

4 Cook for 30–40 minutes, or until the tomatoes are just starting to brown. Serve hot, garnished with a little parsley or fennel, if liked.

——— NUTRITION NOTES ———

Per portion:

Energy	114kcals/476kJ
Protein	3.1g
Fat, total	6.2g
saturated fat	0.9g
Carbohydrate	11.9g
Fibre	4.7g
Sugar	11.8g

——— COOK'S TIP ———

To vary the taste, add seeded, diced red or green peppers to the cabbage in step 1.

Turkish-style New Potato Casserole

This delicious casserole provides plenty of fibre, vitamins, minerals and long-term energy.

INGREDIENTS

Serves 4
60ml/4 tbsp olive oil
1 large onion, chopped
2 small to medium aubergines, cut into small cubes
4 courgettes, cut into small chunks
1 green pepper, and 1 red or yellow pepper, seeded and chopped
115g/4oz/1 cup fresh or frozen peas
115g/4oz green beans
450g/1lb new potatoes, cubed
2.5ml/½ tsp cinnamon
2.5ml/½ tsp paprika
4–5 tomatoes, skinned
400g/14oz can chopped tomatoes
15g/½oz/2 tbsp chopped fresh parsley
3–4 garlic cloves, crushed
350ml/12fl oz/1½ cups vegetable stock
freshly ground black pepper
black olives and fresh parsley, to garnish

1 Heat the oven to 190°C/375°F/ Gas 5. Heat 45ml/3 tbsp of the oil in a heavy-based pan, then add the onion and fry until golden. Add the cubed aubergines to the pan, sauté for 3 minutes, then add the courgettes, peppers, peas, beans and potatoes, together with the spices and freshly ground black pepper.

2 Continue to cook for about 3 minutes, stirring all the time. Transfer the vegetables to a shallow ovenproof dish.

3 Halve the fresh tomatoes and remove their seeds, using a teaspoon. Chop and place in a bowl. Mix in the canned tomatoes, parsley, garlic and the remaining olive oil.

4 Pour the vegetable stock over the aubergine mixture, then spoon the prepared tomato mixture over the top.

5 Cover with foil and bake for 30–45 minutes until the vegetables are tender. Serve hot, garnished with black olives and fresh parsley.

NUTRITION NOTES	
Per portion:	
Energy	270kcals/1131kJ
Protein	9.1g
Fat, total	12.9g
saturated fat	2g
Carbohydrate	31.5g
Fibre	6.5g
Sugar	10.5g

Braised Barley and Vegetables

One of the oldest of cultivated cereals, pot barley has a nutty flavour and slightly chewy texture. It makes a warming and nutritious dish when combined with root vegetables. Barley is said to help digestion and to improve liver function.

INGREDIENTS

Serves 6

225g/8oz/1 cup pearl or
   pot barley
30ml/2 tbsp olive oil
1 large onion, chopped
2 celery sticks, sliced
2 carrots, halved lengthways
   and sliced
225g/8oz swede or turnip, cut
   into 2cm/¾in cubes
225g/8oz potatoes, cut into
   2cm/¾in cubes
475ml/16fl oz/2 cups
   vegetable stock
freshly ground black pepper
celery leaves, to garnish

1 Put the barley in a measuring jug and add water to reach the 600ml/ 1 pint/2½ cup mark. Leave to soak in a cool place for at least 4 hours or preferably overnight.

2 Heat the olive oil in a large pan and fry the onion for about 5 minutes, until softened. Add the sliced celery and carrots and cook for a further 3–4 minutes, or until the onion is starting to brown.

3 Add the barley and its soaking liquid to the pan, then add the cubed swede or turnip, potatoes, vegetable stock and freshly ground black pepper and stir to combine. Bring to the boil, then reduce the heat and cover the pan with a lid.

4 Simmer for 40 minutes, or until most of the stock has been absorbed and the barley is tender. Stir occasionally towards the end of cooking to prevent the barley from sticking to the base of the pan. Serve, garnished with celery leaves.

NUTRITION NOTES	
Per portion:	
Energy	344kcals/1455kJ
Protein	7.4g
Fat, total	8.2g
saturated fat	1.2g
Carbohydrate	64.3g
Fibre	3.1g
Sugar	6.6g

Brown Rice Risotto with Mushrooms

This twist on the classic risotto includes health-giving herbs and brown long grain rice.

INGREDIENTS

Serves 4
15g/½oz/2 tbsp dried porcini
  mushrooms
15ml/1 tbsp olive oil
4 shallots, finely chopped
2 garlic cloves, crushed
250g/9oz/1⅓ cups brown long
  grain rice
900ml/1½ pints/3¾ cups vegetable
  stock
450g/1lb/6 cups mixed
  mushrooms, quartered
30–45ml/2–3 tbsp chopped fresh
  flat leaf parsley
freshly ground black pepper

1 Place the dried porcini mushrooms in a bowl and cover with 150ml/ ¼ pint/⅔ cup hot water. Leave to soak for at least 20 minutes, until the mushrooms are rehydrated.

2 Heat the oil in a large saucepan, add the shallots and garlic and cook gently for 5 minutes, stirring. Drain the porcini, reserving their soaking liquid, and chop roughly. Add the brown rice to the shallot mixture and stir to coat the grains in the oil.

3 Stir the vegetable stock and the porcini soaking liquid into the rice mixture in the saucepan. Bring to the boil, lower the heat and simmer, uncovered, for about 20 minutes or until most of the liquid has been absorbed, stirring frequently.

4 Add all the mushrooms, stir well to combine, and cook the risotto for a further 10–15 minutes more until the liquid has been absorbed.

5 Season to taste with freshly ground black pepper. Stir in the chopped parsley and serve at once.

HEALTH BENEFITS

Brown rice is a good source of B vitamins, and steadies blood sugar levels as it is rich in fibre. It can help to prevent constipation and kidney stones.

NUTRITION NOTES

Per portion:

Energy	284kcals/1202kJ
Protein	8.9g
Fat, total	5.4g
saturated fat	1g
Carbohydrate	53.4g
Fibre	2.9g
Sugar	1.9g

Tomato and Lentil Dhal with Toasted Almonds

Spices have long been recognized for their medicinal qualities, from relieving flatulence to warding off colds and flu. Lentils are a useful source of low-fat protein, providing sustained, long-term energy. They contain significant amounts of B vitamins and are rich in zinc and iron.

INGREDIENTS

Serves 6

30ml/2 tbsp vegetable oil
1 large onion, finely chopped
3 garlic cloves, chopped
1 carrot, diced
10ml/2 tsp cumin seeds
10ml/2 tsp yellow mustard seeds
2.5cm/1in fresh root ginger, grated
10ml/2 tsp ground turmeric
5ml/1 tsp mild chilli powder
5ml/1 tsp garam masala
225g/8oz/1 cup split red lentils
800ml/1¼ pints/3¼ cups water
5 tomatoes, peeled, seeded
    and chopped
juice of 2 limes
60ml/4 tbsp chopped fresh coriander
freshly ground black pepper
25g/1oz/¼ cup flaked almonds,
    toasted, to serve

1 Heat the oil in a heavy-based pan. Sauté the onion for 5 minutes until softened, stirring occasionally. Add the garlic, carrot, cumin and mustard seeds, and ginger. Cook for 5 minutes, stirring, until the seeds pop and the carrot softens slightly.

2 Stir in the ground turmeric, chilli powder and garam masala, and cook for 1 minute or until the flavours begin to mingle, stirring to prevent the spices burning.

3 Add the lentils, water and chopped tomatoes, and season well with freshly ground black pepper. Bring to the boil, then reduce the heat and simmer, covered, for about 45 minutes, stirring occasionally.

4 Stir in the lime juice and 45ml/ 3 tbsp of the coriander. Cook for a further 15 minutes until the lentils are tender. Sprinkle with the remaining coriander and the flaked almonds.

HEALTH BENEFITS

Limes are rich in vitamin C, which can help to improve the absorption of iron.

NUTRITION NOTES

Per portion:

Energy	291kcals/1226kJ
Protein	15.5g
Fat, total	10g
saturated fat	1.1g
Carbohydrate	37g
Fibre	4.6g
Sugar	6.1g

DESSERTS

There is no better way to finish off a meal than with a fresh and

cleansing dessert. Embarking on a detox doesn't have to mean

missing out on treats, and the selection of recipes in this chapter

should keep even the strictest detoxers happy. There is a choice of

fresh and zesty fruit salads, including Exotic Fruit Salad with

Passion Fruit Dressing, and cooked fruit desserts such as Figs and

Pears in Honey, and Apricot and Ginger Compote.

Exotic Fruit Salad with Passion Fruit Dressing

Passion fruit not only makes a superb dressing for any fruit, but is a rich source of vitamin C and betacarotene. Serve this fruit salad soon after preparing to preserve the valuable nutrients.

INGREDIENTS

Serves 6
1 mango
1 papaya
2 kiwi fruit

For the dressing
3 passion fruit
thinly pared rind and juice of
   1 lime
5ml/1 tsp hazelnut or walnut oil
15ml/1 tbsp clear honey

1 Peel the mango, cut it into three slices around the stone, then cut the flesh into chunks and place in a large serving bowl. Peel the papaya and cut it in half. Scoop out the seeds using a spoon, then chop the flesh into similar-size chunks and add to the serving bowl.

2 Cut both ends off each kiwi fruit, then stand them on a board. Using a small sharp knife, slice off the skin. Cut each kiwi fruit in half lengthways, then cut into fairly thick slices. Place in the serving bowl with the other fruit and gently mix together.

3 To make the dressing, cut each passion fruit in half. Scoop the seeds with a teaspoon and place in a sieve set over a small bowl. Press the seeds well to extract all their juices.

4 Lightly whisk the remaining dressing ingredients into the passion fruit juice, then pour the dressing over the fruit. Mix gently to combine. Leave to chill for 1 hour.

COOK'S TIP

A clear, unblended golden honey scented with orange or acacia blossom would be perfect for the dressing. The floral scent will complement the fragrant taste of the tropical fruits.

NUTRITION NOTES

Per portion:

Energy	53kcals/214kJ
Protein	0.8g
Fat, total	0.7g
saturated fat	0.1g
Carbohydrate	11.5g
Fibre	1.9g
Sugar	11.3g

Fruit Platter with Spices

Pineapple, papaya, melon and pomegranates offer an impressive range of detoxifying qualities. There is no need to save this refreshing platter for dessert. Fruit prepared in this way is delicious as an energy-boosting snack during a detox.

INGREDIENTS

Serves 6
1 pineapple
2 papayas
1 small melon
juice of 2 limes
2 pomegranates
ground ginger, to taste
sprigs of mint, to decorate

1 Peel the pineapple. Remove the core and any remaining "eyes", then cut the flesh lengthways into thin wedges. Peel the papayas, cut them in half, and then into thin wedges.

2 Halve the melon and remove the seeds from the middle, using a spoon. Cut it into thin wedges and remove the skin.

3 Arrange the fruit on six individual plates and sprinkle with the lime juice. Cut the pomegranates in half and scoop out the seeds, discarding any pith. Scatter the seeds over the fruit. Serve, sprinkled with a little ginger to taste, and a few sprigs of mint.

VARIATION

The selection of fruit can be varied according to what is available. Apples and bananas make a simple salad, or guavas and mangoes a more exotic combination. Rather than using ginger, simply season with freshly ground black pepper.

HEALTH BENEFITS

Fresh mint has traditionally been used as a cure for indigestion and is also effective in stimulating and cleansing the system.

NUTRITION NOTES

Per portion:

Energy	55kcals/237kJ
Protein	0.8g
Fat, total	0.2g
saturated fat	0.1g
Carbohydrate	13.4g
Fibre	2.2g
Sugar	13.2g

Fresh Fruit Salad

This cleansing fruit salad will help to eliminate toxins.

INGREDIENTS

Serves 6
16–20 strawberries
2 peaches
2 oranges
2 eating apples
30ml/2 tbsp lemon juice
15–30ml/1–2 tbsp orange flower water (optional)
a few fresh mint leaves, to decorate

COOK'S TIP

There are no rules with this fruit salad, and you could use almost any fruit that you like, such as bananas and grapes. Oranges, however, should form the base and apples give a contrast in texture.

1 Hull the strawberries and halve. Pour boiling water over the peaches and leave to stand for 1 minute. Remove from the water, using a slotted spoon, peel away their skin and cut into thick slices.

2 Peel the oranges, removing all the pith, and segment, catching any juice in a small bowl. Peel, core and chop the apples. Place all the fruit in a large serving bowl.

3 Combine the lemon juice, orange flower water, if using, and any reserved orange juice. Pour the fruit juice mixture over the salad and serve decorated with a few fresh mint leaves.

HEALTH BENEFITS

Fruit cleanses and rejuvenates the body, as well as providing vitamins and fibre.

NUTRITION NOTES

Per portion:

Energy	56kcals/234kJ
Protein	1.4g
Fat, total	0.2g
saturated fat	0g
Carbohydrate	13.2g
Fibre	2.4g
Sugar	13.2g

Dried Fruit Salad

This wonderful combination of fresh and dried fruit makes an excellent detox dessert. Both are packed with nutrients and will provide plenty of energy.

INGREDIENTS

Serves 4
115g/4oz/½ cup dried apricots, preferably unsulphured
115g/4oz/½ cup dried peaches, preferably unsulphured
1 pear
1 apple
1 orange
50g/2oz/½ cup blackberries
1 cinnamon stick
45ml/3 tbsp clear unblended honey
30ml/2 tbsp lemon juice
50g/2oz/½ cup raspberries

1 Place the apricots and peaches in a bowl and cover with water. Leave to soak for 1–2 hours until plump, then drain and halve or quarter.

2 Peel and core the pear and apple and cut into cubes. Peel the orange with a sharp knife, removing all the pith, and cut into wedges. Place all the prepared fruit in a large saucepan with the blackberries.

3 Add 600ml/1 pint/2½ cups water, the cinnamon and honey to the pan and bring to the boil. Cover and simmer very gently for 10–12 minutes, then remove the pan from the heat. Stir in the lemon juice and raspberries. Allow the mixture to cool, then pour into a bowl. Cover and chill in the fridge for about 1 hour before serving.

NUTRITION NOTES

Per portion:

Energy	190kcals/794kJ
Protein	3.5g
Fat, total	0.7g
saturated fat	0g
Carbohydrate	45.5g
Fibre	7.2g
Sugar	13.2g

Figs and Pears in Honey

A simple dessert that combines lightly cooked fresh figs and pears. Both fruits are known for their ability to cleanse the system.

INGREDIENTS

Serves 4
1 lemon
90ml/6 tbsp clear honey
1 cinnamon stick
1 cardamom pod
2 pears
8 fresh figs, halved

COOK'S TIP

To vary the flavour, substitute the pears with apples or add a slight kick to the syrup by adding 2.5cm/1in peeled, bruised fresh root ginger in step 2.

---

1 Pare the rind from the lemon using a zester or vegetable peeler, avoiding any of the white pith, then cut into very thin strips.

2 Place the lemon rind, honey, cinnamon stick, cardamom pod and 350ml/12fl oz/1½ cups water in a saucepan and bring to the boil. Boil, uncovered, for about 10 minutes until the liquid has reduced by about half.

NUTRITION NOTES

Per portion:

Energy	147kcals/628kJ
Protein	1.1g
Fat, total	0.4g
saturated fat	0g
Carbohydrate	36.8g
Fibre	3.4g
Sugar	36.8g

3 Cut the pears into eighths, discarding the cores. Place the pears in the syrup, add the halved figs and simmer gently for about 5 minutes until the fruit is tender.

4 Transfer the fruit to a serving bowl. Continue cooking the liquid until syrupy, then discard the cinnamon stick and cardamom pod and pour over the figs and pears.

Strawberries with Passion Fruit Sauce

Fragrant strawberries are always a treat, but they are full of nutrients too. They are rich in antioxidants, including betacarotene and vitamin C, which help to neutralize harmful free radicals in the body.

INGREDIENTS

Serves 4

350g/12oz raspberries, fresh
  or frozen
30ml/2 tbsp honey
1 passion fruit
700g/1½lb small strawberries

1 Place the raspberries and honey in a non-corrosive saucepan and warm over a very gentle heat to release the juices. When the juices start to run, simmer for 5 minutes, stirring occasionally. Set aside and allow the mixture to cool.

2 Halve the passion fruit and, using a teaspoon, carefully scoop out the seeds and juice into a small bowl.

3 Put the raspberries into a food processor or blender, add the passion fruit and blend until smooth.

4 Place the raspberry and passion fruit sauce in a fine nylon sieve and press the purée through to remove the gritty seeds.

5 Spoon some of the sauce over the strawberries and serve. Pass extra sauce separately.

COOK'S TIP

Berry fruits offer their best flavour when served at room temperature, so try to remove strawberries from the fridge at least an hour before you intend to use them.

NUTRITION NOTES

Per portion:

Energy	70kcals/299kJ
Protein	2.7g
Fat, total	0.5g
saturated fat	0.1g
Carbohydrate	14.7g
Fibre	4.2g
Sugar	14.7g

Papaya and Green Grapes with Mint Sauce

Papaya is rich in vitamin C and betacarotene, and also contains calcium, phosphorus and iron. It can be easy to digest and has a tonic effect on the stomach.

INGREDIENTS

Serves 4
2 large papaya
225g/8oz seedless
    green grapes
juice of 3 limes
2.5cm/1in fresh root ginger,
    peeled and finely grated
15ml/1 tbsp clear honey
5 fresh mint leaves, cut into
    thin strips, plus extra whole
    leaves, to decorate

1 Peel the papaya and cut into small cubes, discarding the seeds. Cut the grapes in half.

2 In a bowl, mix together the lime juice, ginger, honey and shredded mint leaves.

3 Add the papaya and grapes and toss well. Leave in a cool place to marinate for 1 hour.

4 Serve in a large dish or individual stemmed glasses, garnished with whole fresh mint leaves.

NUTRITION NOTES	
Per portion:	
Energy	69kcals/289kJ
Protein	0.7g
Fat, total	0.2g
saturated fat	0g
Carbohydrate	17.4g
Fibre	1.9g
Sugar	17.4g

Orange Granita with Strawberries

Although freezing destroys some of the vitamin C content of oranges, this vibrant fruit has many other health-giving qualities, including an ability to tone and stimulate the body and aid digestion.

INGREDIENTS

Serves 4
6 large juicy oranges
350g/12oz ripe strawberries
finely pared strips of orange
    rind, to decorate

1 Juice the oranges and pour into a shallow freezer-proof bowl.

2 Place the bowl in the freezer. Remove after 30 minutes and beat the semi-frozen juice thoroughly with a wooden spoon. Repeat this process at 30-minute intervals over a 4-hour period. This will break the ice crystals down into small particles and prevent the granita freezing solid.

3 Halve the strawberries and arrange them on a serving plate. Scoop the granita into serving glasses, decorate with strips of orange rind and serve immediately with the strawberries.

COOK'S TIP

Granita will keep for up to 3 weeks in the freezer. If you prefer a more tart ice, use sweet pink grapefruits or blood oranges or, alternatively, add a little fresh lemon or lime juice.

NUTRITION NOTES	
Per portion:	
Energy	50kcals/209kJ
Protein	1.5g
Fat, total	0.2g
saturated fat	0g
Carbohydrate	11.3g
Fibre	8.3g
Sugar	11.3g

Lemon Grass Skewers

Grilled fruits make a delicious end to a cleansing meal. The lemon grass skewers give the fruit a subtle lemon tang. The fruits used here make an ideal exotic mix, but almost any soft fruit can be substituted as preferred.

INGREDIENTS

Serves 4

4 long fresh lemon grass stalks
1 mango, peeled, stoned and
  cut into chunks
1 papaya, peeled, seeded and
  cut into chunks
1 star fruit, cut into thick slices
  and halved if large
8 fresh bay leaves
a little nutmeg
60ml/4 tbsp honey
natural live yogurt, to serve

1 Preheat the grill. Cut the top of each lemon grass stalk into a point, then use the back of a knife to bruise each stalk. Thread each stalk with the fruit and bay leaves.

2 Cover a baking sheet in kitchen foil, raising the edges slightly, and lay the skewers on top. Grate nutmeg over each and drizzle with honey. Grill for 5 minutes, until lightly browned.

3 Serve the fruit skewers at once with live natural yogurt.

COOK'S TIP

Only fresh lemon grass will work as skewers for this recipe. It is now possible to buy lemon grass stalks in jars, but they are too soft to use as skewers.

NUTRITION NOTES

Per portion:

Energy	97kcals/416kJ
Protein	0.7g
Fat, total	0.2g
saturated fat	0.1g
Carbohydrate	24.9g
Fibre	2.1g
Sugar	24.7g

Apricot and Ginger Compote

In Chinese medicine, ginger is revered for its health-giving properties. It aids digestion and can help treat colds and flu. Of all the dried fruits, apricots are the richest source of iron. They also provide betacarotene, vitamins A and C, calcium and phosphorus. Live yogurt can relieve gastrointestinal disorders by replacing bacteria in the gut.

INGREDIENTS

Serves 4
350g/12oz/1½ cups dried apricots, preferably unsulphured
4cm/1½in piece fresh root ginger, finely chopped
200g/7oz/scant 1 cup live natural yogurt

1 Cover the dried apricots with boiling water and leave them to soak overnight.

2 Place the apricots and their soaking water in a saucepan, add the fresh root ginger and bring to the boil. Reduce the heat and allow to simmer for 10 minutes until the fruit is soft and plump and the water becomes syrupy. Strain the cooked apricots, reserving the syrup, and discard the ginger.

3 Serve the apricots warm with the reserved syrup and a spoonful or two of live natural yogurt.

COOK'S TIP

Fresh ginger freezes well. Peel the root and store it in a plastic bag in the freezer. You can grate it from frozen, then return the root to the freezer until the next time you need it for a recipe.

NUTRITION NOTES

Per portion:

Energy	166kcals/708kJ
Protein	6.1g
Fat, total	0.9g
saturated fat	0.3g
Carbohydrate	35.7g
Fibre	5.5g
Sugar	35.7g

Dried Fruit Compote

Dried fruit, although slightly higher in sugar – and therefore calories – than fresh, supplies significant amounts of minerals and fibre as well as useful amounts of energy.

INGREDIENTS

Serves 4

350g/12oz/2 cups mixed dried fruits, such as apples, pears, prunes, peaches
1 cinnamon stick
300ml/½ pint/1¼ cups water
65g/2½oz/½ cup raisins
30ml/2 tbsp clear honey
juice of ½ lemon
mint leaves, to decorate

1 Put the mixed dried fruit in a large pan with the cinnamon and water. Heat gently until almost boiling, then cover the pan, lower the heat and cook gently for 12–15 minutes, until the fruit is softened.

2 Remove the pan from the heat, add the raisins and honey and stir gently. Cover the pan with a lid and leave to cool.

3 Once cooled, remove the cinnamon stick and stir in the lemon juice. Transfer the compote to a serving bowl, cover with clear film and keep refrigerated until needed.

4 Before serving, remove the fruit compote from the fridge and allow to return to room temperature. Decorate with a few fresh mint leaves.

----- COOK'S TIP -----

This compote will keep refrigerated for up to a week. If you are following one of the longer detox plans, it is well worth making enough for several servings that you can eat as and when you are ready.

----- NUTRITION NOTES -----

Per portion:

Energy	301kcals/1459kJ
Protein	2.3g
Fat, total	0.4g
saturated fat	0g
Carbohydrate	76.7g
Fibre	2.3g
Sugar	76.7g

Information File

USEFUL ADDRESSES

**Allergy and Environmental
Sensitivity Support and Research
Association (Australia)**
PO Box 298
Ringwood
Victoria 3134
Australia
Tel: (61) 39888 1282

British Nutrition Foundation
High Holborn House
52–54 High Holborn
London WC1V 6RQ
Tel: 020 7404 6504

**Institute for Complementary
Medicine**
PO Box 194
London SE16 1QZ
Tel: 020 7237 5165

Institute for Optimum Nutrition
Blades Court
Deodar Road
London SW15 2NU
Tel: 020 8877 9993

**Ministry of Agriculture, Fisheries
and Food**
Joint Food Safety and Standards Group
Room 306 C
Ergon House, c/o Nobel House
17 Smith Square
London SW1P 3JR
Consumer Helpline: 0345 573012

Pesticides Trust
Eurolink Centre
49 Effra Road
London SW2 1BZ
Tel: 020 7274 8895

**National Association of
Health Stores**
Wayside Cottage
Cuckoo Corner
Urchfont
Devizes SN10 4RA
Tel: 01380 840133

**Royal Society for the Promotion
of Health**
38a St George's Drive
London SW1V 4BH
Tel: 020 7630 0121

**SAFE (Sustainable Agriculture,
Food and Environment) Alliance**
94 White Lion Street
London N1 9PF
Tel: 020 7837 1228

The Soil Association
Bristol House
40-56 Victoria Street
Bristol BS1 6BY
Tel: 01179 290661

FURTHER READING

The Antioxidants
by Richard Passwater – Keats
Publishing Inc, Connecticut

Cleanse Your System
by Amanda Ursell – Thorsons

Fresh Vegetable and Fruit Juices
by N. W. Walker – Norwalk Press

Health Which
Bi-monthly subscription magazine
P.O. Box 44
Hertford SG14 1SH

Natural Detox
by Marie Farquharson – Element

Superjuice
by Michael van Straten – Mitchell
Beazley

Juicing for Health
by Caroline Wheather - Thorsons

The Inside Story on Food and Health
Subscription magazine
Berrydale Publishers
Berrydale House
5 Lawn Road
London NW3 2XS

The Liver Cleansing Diet
by Dr Sandra Cabot – Women's Health
Advisory Service

The Optimum Nutrition Bible
by Patrick Holford – Piatkus

The Organic Directory 1999-2000
by Clive Lichfield – Green Earth
Books

The Sprouting Book
by Ann Wigmore – Avery Publishing
Group Inc

The Wheatgrass Book
by Ann Wigmore – Avery Publishing
Group Inc

What the Label Doesn't Tell You
by Sue Dibb – Thorsons

ORGANIC FOODS

Nutricia
Whitehorse Business Park
Trowbridge
Wiltshire BA14 OXQ
Tel: 01225 711677

Organics Direct
7 Willow Street
London EC2A 4BH
Tel: 020 7729 2828

Holland & Barrett
Branches throughout the UK

Index